WASHINGTON
Wild Roads

80 Scenic Drives
to Camping, Hiking Trails, and Adventures

SEABURY BLAIR JR.

SASQUATCH BOOKS
SEATTLE

This book is dedicated to my trusty 1979
Subaru, the first vehicle that carried me
thousands of bumpy miles on wild roads

Printed in the United States of America

Published by Sasquatch Books
18 17 16 15 14 13 12   9 8 7 6 5 4 3 2 1

Front cover photograph: © 2011 by JD Hascup
Cover design: Sasquatch Books
Interior design and composition: Sarah Plein
Back cover and interior photographs: Seabury Blair Jr.; USDA Forest
Service/Melissa Days (page 88)
Maps: Marlene Blair

Library of Congress Cataloging-in-Publication Data is available.

ISBN-13: 978-1-57061-815-4

Sasquatch Books
1904 Third Avenue, Suite 710
Seattle, WA 98101
(206) 467-4300
www.sasquatchbooks.com
custserv@sasquatchbooks.com

WASHINGTON
Wild Roads

CONTENTS

DRIVES AT A GLANCE

Flatlanders Welcome

NO.	DRIVE NAME	RATING	DISTANCE	ROAD CONDITION	ROAD GRADE
1	Lake Cushman Road	◉◉◉	16.2 miles	Good	Moderate
4	Dosewallips River Road	◉◉◉	10.1 miles	Good	Moderate
10	Oil City Road	◉	10.7 miles	Fair	Moderate
11	Upper Hoh Road	◉◉◉	18.5 miles	Good	Flat
12	Lake Quinault Loop	◉◉◉	28.4 miles	Good	Flat
13	Campbell Tree Grove	◉◉◉	23.3 miles	Good	Moderate
14	Green Mountain Road	◉	4.1 miles	Good	Steep
17	Hannegan Pass Road	◉◉◉◉	5.3 miles	Fair	Moderate
19	Skyline Divide Road	◉◉◉	12.7 miles	Fair	Moderate
21	Lake Shannon	◉◉	15.5 miles	Good/Poor	Steep
22	Baker Lake Road	◉◉◉	26.1 miles	Good	Moderate
25	Chewuch River Road	◉◉◉◉	27.6 miles	Excellent/Good	Moderate
26	Nice Campground	◉◉◉	13.4 miles	Good	Moderate
28	Salmon Meadows	◉◉◉◉	8.5 miles	Good	Moderate
31	Tonga Ridge	◉◉	11.2 miles	Good	Moderate
32	Beckler River Road	◉◉	15.2 miles	Good	Moderate
34	Miller River Road	◉◉◉	10.2 miles	Good	Moderate
35	Iron Goat Wayside	◉◉	6.6 miles	Good	Moderate
39	Little Wenatchee River Road	◉◉	15.4 miles	Good	Moderate
40	White River Road	◉◉	10.5 miles	Good	Moderate
41	Chiwawa River Road	◉◉◉◉	25.2 miles	Good	Moderate
42	Icicle Creek Road	◉◉◉◉	14.5 miles	Good	Moderate
48	Tacoma Pass	◉◉	12.1 miles	Good	Moderate
50	Kachess Lake	◉◉◉	5.4 miles	Excellent	Flat
51	East Kachess Lake Road	◉	4.8 miles	Good/Poor	Flat
53	Cooper Lake Road	◉◉◉◉◉	5.7 miles	Good	Steep
54	Taneum Creek Road	◉◉◉	15.0 miles	Good	Moderate
55	Yakima Canyon Road	◉◉◉◉	25.4 miles	Excellent	Moderate
60	Little Naches River	◉◉◉	16.1 miles	Excellent	Moderate
65	Takhlakh Lake	◉◉◉◉◉	32.3 miles	Good	Moderate
66	South Fork Tieton River	◉◉	12.6 miles	Fair	Moderate
67	Rimrock Lake Loop	◉◉◉	16.6 miles	Excellent	Moderate

69	Oak Creek Wildlife Area	⚙⚙⚙	5.8 miles	Fair	Moderate
70	Skate Creek Road	⚙⚙⚙	23.0 miles	Good	Moderate
72	Mowich Lake	⚙⚙⚙⚙⚙	16.5 miles	Fair/Poor	Steep
73	Crab Creek	⚙⚙⚙⚙	19.8 miles	Good	Flat
74	Hanford Reach	⚙⚙⚙	5.7 miles	Fair	Moderate
75	Turnbull Wildlife Refuge	⚙⚙⚙⚙	5.9-mile loop	Good	Flat
78	Browns Lake	⚙⚙⚙⚙	11.7 miles	Good	Moderate
79	Flowery Trail Road	⚙⚙⚙	27.4 miles	Excellent	Steep

Sightseeing OK

NO.	DRIVE NAME	RATING	DISTANCE	ROAD CONDITION	ROAD GRADE
2	Forest Road 24	⚙⚙	19.0 miles	Fair	Moderate
3	Mount Ellinor Road	⚙⚙⚙⚙	18.4 miles	Fair	Steep
5	Big Quilcene Road	⚙⚙⚙	16.4 miles	Good	Steep
6	Bon Jon Pass	⚙⚙	27.5 miles	Good	Steep
8	Hurricane Ridge Road	⚙⚙⚙⚙⚙	19.3 miles	Excellent	Steep
15	Dewatto Loop	⚙⚙⚙	75.4 miles	Fair	Steep
16	Mount Baker Highway	⚙⚙⚙⚙	10.2 miles	Excellent	Steep
20	Mount Baker Vista	⚙⚙⚙⚙	9.0 miles	Fair	Steep
24	Banker Pass	⚙⚙	12.6 miles	Fair	Steep
27	Baldy Pass	⚙⚙⚙⚙	25.0 miles	Good	Steep
29	Tiffany Meadows	⚙⚙⚙	30.7 miles	Good	Steep
30	Sinlahekin Valley	⚙⚙⚙⚙	14.0+ miles	Good	Moderate
33	Lake Elizabeth	⚙⚙⚙	7.7 miles	Fair	Moderate
36	Old Cascade Highway	⚙⚙⚙	2.9 miles	Fair	Steep
37	Nason Ridge	⚙⚙⚙	4.0 miles	Good	Steep
38	Rainy Creek Road	⚙⚙⚙⚙	9.3 miles	Good	Steep
43	Teanaway River Road	⚙⚙⚙⚙⚙	23.6 miles	Fair	Moderate
44	Swauk Pass West	⚙	4.0 miles	Fair	Moderate
46	Old Blewett Pass Highway	⚙⚙⚙	9.8 miles	Fair	Steep
47	Liberty to Swauk Pass	⚙⚙⚙⚙	14.0 miles	Good	Steep
49	Lost Lake	⚙⚙⚙⚙	5.9 miles	Good	Steep
52	Tucquala Meadows	⚙⚙⚙⚙⚙	28.9 miles	Good/Fair	Steep
58	Sunrise Road	⚙⚙⚙⚙⚙	14.8 miles	Excellent	Steep
59	Raven Roost	⚙⚙⚙⚙	16.7 miles	Fair	Steep
61	Boulder Cave	⚙⚙⚙	22.3 miles	Good/Fair	Steep
62	Canteen Flats	⚙⚙⚙⚙	7.5 miles	Good/Poor	Steep
63	McDaniel Lake	⚙⚙	12.0 miles	Good	Steep

64	Windy Ridge	✹✹✹✹	36.1 miles	Good	Steep
68	Bethel Ridge Road	✹✹✹	25.4 miles	Good	Steep
71	Towhead Gap Loop	✹✹✹✹✹	26.3 miles	Good	Steep
76	Mount Spokane Road	✹✹✹✹	22.5 miles	Good	Steep
77	Mystic Lake	✹✹✹	24.6 miles	Good	Moderate

White Knuckles

NO.	DRIVE NAME	RATING	DISTANCE	ROAD CONDITION	ROAD GRADE
7	Deer Park Road	✹✹✹✹✹	17.2 miles	Good	Extremely steep
9	Obstruction Point Road	✹✹✹✹✹	7.7 miles	Good	Steep
45	Haney Meadows	✹✹✹✹	8.2 miles	Good/Poor	Extremely steep
56	Sun Top Road	✹✹✹✹✹	6.8 miles	Fair	Steep
57	Corral Pass	✹✹✹✹	5.5 miles	Fair	Extremely steep
80	Salmo Mountain Lookout	✹✹✹✹✹	20.9 miles	Good	Steep

Valium Prescribed

NO.	DRIVE NAME	RATING	DISTANCE	ROAD CONDITION	ROAD GRADE
18	Twin Lakes Road	✹✹✹✹✹	6.6 miles	Good/Poor	Extremely steep
23	Hart's Pass Road	✹✹✹✹✹	19.2 miles	Good	Extremely steep

INTRODUCTION

A funny thing happened on my weekly dash to the trailhead in the Belching Beast, my trusty Ford pickup: I began to slow down and enjoy the scenery. For many years, the Beast and I raced to the trailhead, eating forest road dust from hikers who got an earlier start than me. I learned early on in my adventures that no matter how soon I hit the road, somebody always hits it sooner.

It was this lesson, combined with the fact that my creaky knees now rival those of the Tin Man in *The Wizard of Oz*, that first caused me to ease the pressure on the Beast's accelerator pedal and start looking around. With good health and fortune, I'll never stop walking the wilderness pathways. But more importantly, getting close to Mother Nature—even if it is only behind a steering wheel—is to my way of thinking the ultimate goal.

The Sunday Drive is disappearing, largely because the destination is more important than the adventure of getting there. As that splendid movie *Cars* pointed out, most people no longer drive for simple pleasure. The sad truth is, very few roads in Washington or any other state are built for driving pleasure. They are constructed primarily to get us safely and quickly from Point A to Point B. We speed from home to the office, the garage to the grocery, or the carpool lot to the trailhead. All of our attention is focused on getting the kids to the soccer pitch, and may the dolt in the big SUV who just cut you off rot in hell.

Yes, there are such things as backroads and country lanes that make operating a motor vehicle a more pleasant experience. These roads and secondary highways serve up some scenery and provide a chance to enjoy the trip. You'll find a number of guides that point them out to you. But they aren't the kind of thoroughfare where, should you see a deer grazing near the shoulder, you might stop in the middle of the road to watch without fear of getting rear-ended. Worse, should the deer cross the road, it is likely many motorists will be going too fast to stop.

So I'm happy to report that some roads—I call them "wild"—insist, by the quality of their surface or the scenery they traverse, that you slow down. They lead you to the edge of wilderness, through forests so tall the sky is a narrow slot overhead, up mountainsides to flower-filled meadows and August snow-fields, across sagebrush prairies and stark basalt coulees. They are the last examples of the byways that existed everywhere seven or eight decades ago, roads built simply to be enjoyed.

Ironically, you'll find most wild roads in Washington's seven national forests, and most were not originally built for recreation. They were used—and continue to be used today—by people who make a living in our forests. So it is essential to remember that while we're on our way to the picnic or campground, we'll be sharing the road with others whose livelihood depends on it. In most, if not all cases, signs announce active logging or even road closures.

That's fine by me. As you'll see by looking at any state road atlas, there are literally hundreds of wild roads in Washington. What follows here are 80 of the very best, and I hope you'll find them as enjoyable as I do. Get an early start, or you'll be eating my dust.

USING THIS GUIDE

The tabular matter at the beginning of each drive is intended to give you specific and quick information that can help you decide whether you might like to ride this road. The information includes:

Road Number and Name

Most of the roads in this guide begin at junctions with main highways or byways in various regions of the state. For the most part, the byways are listed along each highway corridor from west to east. You'll find recommended roads on the Olympic and Kitsap Peninsulas, the Mount Baker Highway (State Route 542), the North Cascades Highway (State Route 20), Stevens Pass Highway (US Route 2), Swauk Pass Highway (State Routes 970 and 97), Snoqualmie Pass (Interstate 90), the Chinook Pass Highway (State Route 410), White Pass Highway (US Highway 12), and the Road to Paradise (State Route 706) on the south side of Mount Rainier. I've recommended only eight of hundreds of beautiful roads in Eastern Washington, simply because motorists from the western part of the state aren't likely to drive so far for a Sunday outing. And some Sunday drivers on the eastern side of the state would just as soon keep their favorite roads to themselves.

Overall Rating

This is purely a subjective attempt to rank the roads from the very best (5 wheels) to those that aren't quite so good (1 wheel), but are far better than the byways you won't find outlined in this guide. I tend to rank the roads with splendid vistas above those that snake through deep forest or along river bottoms, so if you prefer that kind of road, feel free to assume I'm a dunderheaded fool and ignore my rating altogether.

Distance

The driving distance is listed one-way to a recommended turnaround point. The turnaround point may be at the end of the road, or the end of pavement, or at a point where I encountered washboarding or potholes that would shake the bolts off a Land Rover or swallow a Hummer.

Road Surface

I've listed roads that are paved, graded gravel, graded dirt, or not maintained. Many of the roads in this guide start as paved byways and turn to gravel or dirt at some point along the way. In such cases, you'll see "Paved/Graded dirt," or "Paved/Graded gravel."

The only road that is not officially maintained in this guide is the Twin Lakes Road, off the Mount Baker Highway 542. Signs are posted where the maintenance ends at the Tomyhoi Lakes trailhead.

Road Condition

This is a tough one, because conditions on most of these roads can change from month to month, depending upon traffic load, weather, and the road manager's maintenance schedule. Thus take my rating with a cup of caution, and consult with the friendly land manager whose telephone number is listed in the Land Manager/Contact entry.

Drivers on roads described as "Excellent" will find surfaces free of potholes and washboarding. "Good" roads will be those with few bumps and lumps; a "Fair" road is one you'll navigate slowly around holes and jiggle intermittently from washboard surfaces. A road that is rated "Poor" is a rough road indeed, and you'll find few in that category in this guide.

Road Grade

Here you'll discover what the steepest section of the drive will be. Many wild roads have sections, often not terribly long, with grades that put some two-wheel-drive cars to the test. Road grades are rated as "Extremely steep," which might compare to some of the steeper Seattle streets on Queen Anne or Capitol Hill; or "Steep," which could be found on the lesser Seattle hills. A grade rated "Moderate" would be one you'd find on a state highway, while "Flat"—as I'm certain you'll guess—is really no grade at all.

Pucker Factor

For certain logging truck drivers, road rallye pros, and perhaps destruction derby pilots, the Pucker Factor is a myth. But if you find yourself on a single-lane road a couple of hundred feet above a rock-walled river canyon, and some geek in a Hummer is headed toward you at the speed of sound, I'm guessing this rating might be helpful. I trust the ratings "Valium prescribed," "White knuckles," "Sightseeing OK," and "Flatlanders welcome" are self-explanatory.

Accessible

The section tells you when the road is open for vehicle travel. Some roads can be driven all year; many can be driven in spring, summer, or fall; and some can only be driven in the summer and fall or in the spring and summer. Roads rated for "Summer only" driving would be those that are closed by snow or gated during certain seasons to protect wildlife.

Land Manager/Contact

This section will include a telephone number and website for the agency that manages the land your road traverses. The National Forest Service manages most wild roads in this guide, and contact numbers will list the ranger district through which the byway passes. As I mentioned earlier, it is a good idea to check with the land manager before heading to any road to make sure conditions have not changed since this guide was prepared.

A note about the websites: the National Forest Service has apparently changed all of the URLs for national forests into incredibly long and complicated addresses, which would be impossible to duplicate without a copy function. For example, the old URL for Mount Baker–Snoqualmie National Forest was www.fs.usda.gov/mbs. Are you ready for the new address?

www.fs.usda.gov/wps/portal/fsinternet/!ut/p/c4/04_SB8K8xLLM9MSSz Py8xBz9CP0os3gjAwhwtDDw9_AI8zPwhQoY6BdkOyoCAPkATlA!/?ss =110605&navtype=BROWSEBYSUBJECT&cid=FSE_003853&navid=0910 00000000000&pnavid=null&position=BROWSEBYSUBJECT&ttype=main &pname=Mt.%20Baker-Snoqualmie%20National%20Forest-%20Home

I'm using the old URLs here. You'll automatically be transferred to the new site.

Trailheads

This section is where you'll find a list of the trails that begin along a road. I've tried to list them in the order they will appear as you drive toward the turn-around point or the end of a loop. The trailheads will also be shown on the drive map, and in some cases, more than one trail starts at the same trailhead.

Included in a few of the drives are brief descriptions of the trails, especially the shorter, easier walks where motorists might want to stretch their legs. If you see a trail that looks interesting but you didn't bring your hiking boots, I'd suggest you make note of it and return later with a proper hiking guide (such as any in the Day Hike! series) that describes the trek in detail.

Campgrounds

Travelers looking to get off the interstate, or seeking a quieter spot to pitch a tent or enjoy a picnic, will find this section helpful. Most—if not all—of the developed public campgrounds are listed here in the order they appear along the route. The majority have amenities such as water systems or wells, some type of restroom facilities, picnic tables, and fire rings. Many have separate areas for day-use.

"Diverse" camping—where few amenities are provided and numbers rarely designate sites—can be found along some of the drives. Often these areas are better than developed campgrounds for day-use, and permits may not be necessary. Look for "Northwest Forest Pass Required" or "Discover Pass Required" signs.

Detailed descriptions of the campgrounds aren't provided, although I do mention some of my favorites in passing. If a particular campsite looks interesting to you when planning your drive, visit the website listed in the Land Manager/Contact section. Another excellent source for Forest Service campgrounds is www.forestcamping.com.

Notes

Here you'll find any information that could help you choose which road you'd like to drive. I'll note roads that are particularly dusty in the summer, or muddy when they get wet, or provide good wildlife-watching opportunities.

If a fee or pass is required to gain access to the road or park at trailheads or picnic areas along the way, I'll note it here. Generally, you'll need a Washington State Discover Pass ($10 daily, $30–$35 annually) for state parks and Department of Natural Resources and Washington Department of Fish and Wildlife lands *only* if you plan to stop for a picnic or admire the view for an extended length of time; a Northwest Forest Pass ($5 daily, $30 annually) for national forest parking areas with toilet facilities in Washington and Oregon; or one of several National Parks passes ($15/7-day, $30/annual at Olympic and Rainier National Parks). Adults 62 years old or older qualify for a $10 lifetime pass allowing them entrance into all federally managed areas, such as national parks, historical sites, forests, and the like.

The Drive

This section will attempt to summarize the highlights of the road in one or two sentences.

Getting There

This contains specific directions for finding the junction of the drive's starting point and a major highway, with distance from the nearest town. I've included GPS information on the location of the road and its junction with the highway or main road. In a few cases, when my Garmin eTrex failed me, the GPS information was taken from the National Geographic TOPO! program.

The Road

Here you'll find a detailed description of the thoroughfare from beginning to the end or recommended turnaround point, including mileages from its beginning. Roadside features I'll describe might include viewpoints, lakes or meadows, likely spots for wildlife viewing, campgrounds, picnic areas, or hiking trailheads.

Maps

The maps appearing in this guide were created from United States Geological Survey (USGS) quadrangles and are intended to give you a graphic description of the routes you will be driving. Although every effort has been made to make them as accurate as possible, they should not be used for navigation unless they are supplemented with National Forest Motor Vehicle Use Maps, available at most National Forest Ranger Station information centers. Wild roads outside forest boundaries can be found on USGS maps.

When scale permitted, several drives were combined on a single

MAP LEGEND	
90	Interstate Highway
101	U.S. Highway
3	State Highway
	Local Road
1	Paved Wild Road
··············	Unpaved Wild Road
•	Community
⋀	Campground
(TH)	Trailhead
▲▲▲	Mountain
╱	Waterfalls
— — — —	Boundary
∼	River, Creek

map. Numbers and names indicate each drive that is described in the text that follows. For example, the map on page 2 displays drives #1, #2, and #3 in this guide.

Note also that trailheads shown on the map may not always equal the number of trailheads listed in the drive description. In such cases, several trails begin at the same location. For example, the map for drive #7, Deer Park Road, on page 22 indicates a single trailhead where three trails begin.

While nearly all of the maps differentiate between paved and gravel roads, several thoroughfares alternate between gravel and short sections of pavement at bridges or around curves where uphill traffic might carve potholes or result in a washboard road. One such road leading to the Mount Baker Vista is shown as pavement to the Heliotrope Ridge Trailhead on the map on page 60, but it is actually a mix of pavement and gravel to that point.

Seeing which roads are paved or gravel is one of a number of features you'll find on the maps. You'll also find symbols for trailheads, campgrounds, nearby mountains, and others. Use the legend above to interpret the maps.

DRIVING WILD ROADS

Most of the roads in this guide come as close to the wilderness as you can get without getting out of your vehicle. All but a very few of these byways can be navigated in a two-wheel-drive passenger car, although a four-wheel- or all-wheel-drive vehicle with higher ground clearance might add a margin of comfort for some motorists.

Since these roads traverse large areas of unpopulated land, you are likely to find that cell phone service is spotty, at best. That reason alone might be enough to convince you to drive with added caution on wild roads. Every year, forest rangers or other drivers happen across unfortunate motorists on wild roads with flat tires or other difficulties, unable to call for help and perhaps a full day's hike to civilization. While driving the roads included here, I met a couple at the Nason Ridge trailhead off Forest Road 6700 who had just helped push a tourist's rental car out of a snowbank in July. Had they not happened along, the tourists might have spent a cold night in their car.

The prudent course is to prepare for such situations ahead of time. Make sure your spare tire is in good condition and that you can change it if necessary. Pack a first-aid kit in the car, along with a blanket or sleeping bag and perhaps a can or two of nonperishable food and a water container. National Forest Service pamphlets say motorists should plan to encounter rocks and boulders, road washouts, downed trees, and brush encroaching on the roadway.

Plan to carry an axe or big pruning saw, shovel, gloves, and extra fuel. Expect to encounter logging trucks, even on roads that aren't posted "Logging Use Only." Watch for turnouts on one-lane roads and be prepared to stop and wait if you see oncoming traffic. When passing an oncoming vehicle on a wild road, one vehicle should always stop while the other passes slowly. Though not required, it is a good idea to increase your visibility by turning on your headlights.

Most wild roads are posted with speed limits, which vary but seldom exceed 35 miles per hour. On gravel and dirt roads, 25 miles per hour is usually a safe speed, but sharp curves, steep grades, potholes, washboarding, or rocky surfaces can slow your progress to 10 or even 5 miles per hour.

During the summer months, dust is usually the biggest driving nuisance, if not hazard. Vehicles stir up clouds of it, making both visibility and breathing difficult. Forest Service pamphlets warn drivers to never follow in another vehicle's dust cloud, and the best solution is to pull over and wait until visibility is restored. Driving gravel or dirt roads early in the morning is a good way to avoid getting dusted and has the added plus of being the best time for spotting wildlife. On forest roads on the wet west side of the state, shaded roads can remain dust-free for as many as one or two days following a rain-soaking.

Always carry a map of the area because the maps in this guide are intended to give you a general idea of the country you are traversing, but should not be relied upon for navigation. The best maps are black and white National Forest Motor Vehicle Use Maps, available for $5 at most ranger stations. They are extremely accurate and if I have a single quibble with them, it is that my ancient eyes can no longer read the tiny, itsy-bitsy road identification numbers on the map. In addition to the Vehicle Use Maps, colored National Forest Maps can be purchased as well.

It's not a good idea to rely solely on a vehicle's onboard GPS navigation system, as not all wild roads could be included in the system. Some roads in deep forests may not be visible to satellites.

Now, fire up whatever you call your Belching Beast, and head for the wild roads of Washington. Pass with care!

OLYMPIC AND KITSAP PENINSULAS

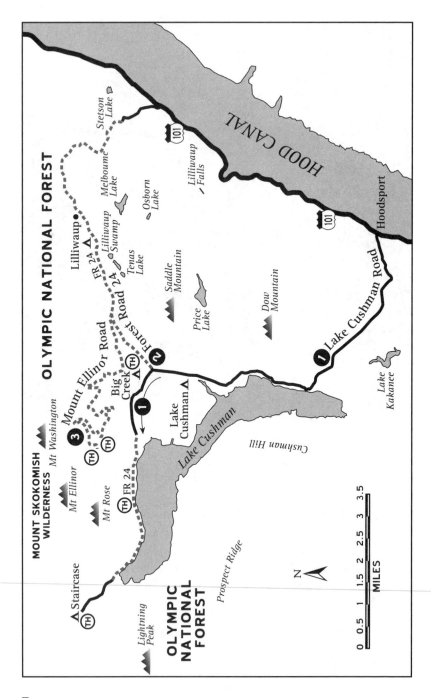

1. Lake Cushman Road

RATING	✹✹✹
DISTANCE	16.2 miles
ROAD SURFACE	Paved/Graded gravel
ROAD CONDITION	Good
ROAD GRADE	Moderate
PUCKER FACTOR	Flatlanders welcome
ACCESSIBLE	Spring–fall
LAND MANAGER/CONTACT	Olympic National Forest, Hood Canal Ranger District, (360) 765-2200, www.fs.fed.us/r6/olympic
TRAILHEADS	Big Creek Loop, Mount Rose, Four Stream, Staircase Loop, Wagonwheel Lake
CAMPGROUNDS	Cushman, Big Creek, Staircase
NOTES	Northwest Forest Pass ($5 daily, $30 annually) required. Entry fee ($15/7-day, $30 annually) required at Staircase.

The Drive

Here's a pleasant thoroughfare along a big lake past picnic areas and swimming holes to the North Fork of the Skokomish River and Olympic National Park.

Getting There

Follow Highway 101 to Hoodsport, on the west shore of Hood Canal, and turn left on the Lake Cushman Road, Highway 119. GPS location: N47°24.381'; W123°08.444'

The Road

If you're looking for a quick escape from the city, this just might be the drive for you. Take a picnic lunch, a bathing suit, a pair of hiking boots, a camera, and binoculars for watching the elk herd that usually hangs out near the Olympic National Park boundary at the north end of Lake Cushman.

The original lake, called by some early settlers the "Devil Cush," was a broad extension of the Skokomish River and the site of an old resort that was flooded when the dam was completed in 1926. It was here that the exploring party led by Lt. Joseph O'Neil set off to cross the Olympic Mountains in 1890.

From Hoodsport, the paved road climbs the hills overlooking Hood Canal, passing a number of private residences before rounding a corner and gaining a view of the lake at about **5.0** miles. You're likely to be as impressed with

Mount Lincoln, just west of Mount Ellinor and Mount Washington, looks down on Lake Cushman.

the view of Mounts Ellinor and Washington above as you are with the clear water of the lake below. The road has a number of private driveways on both sides, but there's no confusing the main byway as it twists down to forested flats above the lake and at **7.0** miles, passes the entrance to the Cushman Campground, once a state park now privately operated.

The road now leaves the lake and travels north, and drivers might imagine they're going to bump into Mount Ellinor, directly in front of them. Instead, the road takes a bend and arrives at a junction with Forest Road 24, **9.3** miles from Hoodsport. Turn left here, passing Big Creek Campground and the trailhead for a loop hike that climbs up the Big Creek canyon and back. The road climbs a low hill to the northwest and passes a junction with the Lake Cushman Village Road on the left. Here's where the pavement ends, **11.0** miles from Hoodsport.

The road drops to a level just above the lake and follows the shoreline underneath the steep forested hillside of Mount Rose, passing a number of pullouts and picnic spots above the lake. The first is about **12.0** miles from Hoodsport and a Northwest Forest Pass is required if you plan to park at any of the picnic areas. At **12.2** miles, you'll pass the Mount Rose trailhead on your right. This steep loop trail climbs across the rocky summit of the mountain above.

Around **14.5** miles, toward the end of the lake, the road hugs the shoreline underneath cliffs exposed by two wildfires that eliminated most of the vegetation anchoring huge rocks, and closed the road to public access for a year. The road is roughest in this section as it passes through Bear Gulch at the north end of the lake. The nice picnic area and swimming hole is **15.0** miles from Hoodsport.

Round a corner and in 0.2 mile, you'll encounter a paved road as you enter Olympic National Park. Look to the river flats on the left, where elk can often be seen. The Staircase Entry Station, where you may be asked to pay a $15 fee, is **16.0** miles from Hoodsport, and the road ends at the Staircase Ranger Station another 0.2 mile beyond. You'll find an auto campground and trails leading up the North Fork of the Skokomish River at Staircase, as well as a short wheelchair-accessible loop trail.

2. Forest Road 24

RATING	⊕⊛
DISTANCE	19.0 miles
ROAD SURFACE	Paved/Graded gravel
ROAD CONDITION	Fair
ROAD GRADE	Moderate
PUCKER FACTOR	Sightseeing OK
ACCESSIBLE	Spring–fall
LAND MANAGER/CONTACT	Olympic National Forest, Hood Canal Ranger District, (360) 765-2200, www.fs.fed.us/r6/olympic
CAMPGROUNDS	Lilliwaup
NOTES	Forested sections stay wet and muddy long after rain

The Drive

You might save this outing for a rainy day when wildlife-watching or cruising through timberland is the main reason for a road trip.

Getting There

Follow Highway 101 to Hoodsport, on the west shore of Hood Canal, and turn left on the Lake Cushman Road, Highway 119. (See map on page 2.) GPS location: N47°24.381'; W123°08.444'

The Road

From Hoodsport, the paved road climbs the hills overlooking Hood Canal, passing a number of private residences before rounding a corner and gaining a view of the lake at about **5.0** miles. You're likely to be as impressed with the view of Mounts Ellinor and Washington above as you are with the clear water of the lake below. The road has a number of private driveways on both sides, but there's no confusing the main byway as it twists down to forested flats above the lake and at **7.0** miles, passes the entrance to the Cushman Campground, once a state park now privately operated.

The road now leaves the lake and travels north, and drivers might imagine they're going to bump into Mount Ellinor, directly in front of them. Instead, the road takes a bend and arrives at a junction with Forest Road 24, **9.3** miles from Hoodsport.

Turn right at this junction, where the pavement ends, and continue through a young forest of fir and alder. At **10.6** miles, the road crosses into the

Mount Lincoln sits above Lake Cushman.

Hood Canal State Forest and in another 0.3 mile, arrives at a junction with the Mount Ellinor Road, Forest Road 2419. Stay right and pass a Department of Natural Resources campground on the left. This campground, Lilliwaup, was closed in the spring of 2011, but may be reopened by now and if so, you'll need a Discover Pass ($10 daily, $30–$35 annually) if you stop here.

Next, you'll pass an unsigned road junction **12.9** miles from Hoodsport on the right and in another 0.4 mile, pass an intersection with Forest Road 2441. Keep right here and drive through a clear-cut on your right, where you might spot deer or elk. You'll be heading downhill toward the west shore of Hood Canal and in the spring, you might spot vultures riding wind currents along the bluff. Stay left at the next road junction, **14.9** miles from Hoodsport. The road passes through another clear-cut and follows a power line north at **16.3** miles.

At **16.7** miles, turn right at the junction with Forest Road 2480 and pass a junction with the Olympic Trails Road on the left, **18.6** miles from Hoodsport. In another 0.3 mile, you'll join Highway 101 at Jorsted Creek. Turn right to return to Hoodsport.

3. Mount Ellinor Road

RATING	❀❀❀❀
DISTANCE	18.4 miles
ROAD SURFACE	Paved/Graded gravel
ROAD CONDITION	Fair
ROAD GRADE	Steep
PUCKER FACTOR	Sightseeing OK
ACCESSIBLE	Summer, fall
LAND MANAGER/CONTACT	Olympic National Forest, Hood Canal Ranger District, (360) 765-2200, www.fs.fed.us/r6/olympic
TRAILHEADS	Lower and Upper Mount Ellinor
NOTES	Northwest Forest Pass ($5 daily, $30 annually) required

The Drive

The road to the upper trailhead on Mount Ellinor makes a great sightseeing destination for views of the Hood Canal and Lake Cushman. You might glimpse mountain goats on the slopes of Ellinor above.

Getting There

Follow Highway 101 to Hoodsport, on the west shore of Hood Canal, and turn left on the Lake Cushman Road, Highway 119. (See map on page 2.) GPS location: N47°24.381'; W123°08.444'

The Road

From Hoodsport, the paved road climbs the hills overlooking Hood Canal, passing a number of private residences before rounding a corner and gaining a view of the lake at about **5.0** miles. You're likely to be as impressed with the view of Mounts Ellinor and Washington above as you are with the clear water of the lake below. The road has a number of private driveways on both sides, but there's no confusing the main byway as it twists down to forested flats above the lake and at **7.0** miles, passes the entrance to the Cushman Campground, once a state park now privately operated.

The road now leaves the lake and travels north, and drivers might imagine they're going to bump into Mount Ellinor, directly in front of them. Instead, the road takes a bend and arrives at a junction with Forest Road 24, **9.3** miles from Hoodsport. Turn right at the junction, where the pavement ends, and drive 1.6 miles to the Mount Ellinor Road, Forest Road 2419, and turn left.

The Mount Ellinor Road ends with a steep trail to the summit of the mountain, with views of the interior Olympic Mountains.

The road begins climbing immediately above a young forest of fir and alder. Views of the Big Creek canyon below and the "Big Bend" country of Hood Canal expand as you climb higher into the mountains and cross Skinwood Creek, **13.5** miles from Hoodsport. Stay left at a junction with Forest Road 2464, just beyond. The road winds around the hillside and crosses two forks of Big Creek at **14.5** miles, then climbs to a sharp switchback where a road leads to the left for spectacular views down to Lake Cushman and beyond. You'll climb to the right where, at **15.6** miles, you'll pass the Lower Mount Ellinor trailhead on the left. This nice forested trail was once the beginning of the climber's route up the mountain.

The road continues past the trailhead through reforested areas where you can look up at Mount Washington on the right and Mount Ellinor to the left. Reach a junction with a road leading to the base of Mount Washington, **17.2** miles from Hoodsport, and turn left, climbing the steepest part of the road and arriving at the Upper Mount Ellinor trailhead, **18.3** miles from Hoodsport. The Upper trailhead parking area, where you'll find a restroom, is a busy place in the summer as hikers head for the 5,944-foot summit. This trailhead is rarely free of snow until late spring.

If you've brought your binoculars, you can look up the mountain to a high meadow where the climber's trail can be seen angling toward the summit. Look here for mountain goats, or scan the rocky slopes to the north and east.

4. Dosewallips River Road

RATING	⚙⚙⚙
DISTANCE	10.1 miles
ROAD SURFACE	Paved/Graded gravel
ROAD CONDITION	Good
ROAD GRADE	Moderate
PUCKER FACTOR	Flatlanders welcome
ACCESSIBLE	Year-round
LAND MANAGER/CONTACT	Olympic National Forest, Hood Canal Ranger District, (360) 765-2200, www.fs.fed.us/r6/olympic
TRAILHEADS	Tunnel Creek
NOTES	Good wildlife-watching possibilities

The Drive

This forest thoroughfare travels along the edge of the tumbling Dosewallips River, which, more than a decade ago, bit a chunk out of the road the size of a football field and spit it into Hood Canal 10 miles downstream.

Getting There

Follow Highway 101 along the shore of Hood Canal to Brinnon and turn west onto the Dosewallips River Road. GPS location: N47°41.923'; W122°53.804'

The Road

The Dosewallips River Road once stretched 16.0 miles upriver to Olympic National Park and an auto campground, giving hikers, anglers, and nature lovers access to ancient forests. Mother Nature cut off the last 6.0 miles of the road in 2002 with a rainstorm and washout, closing two auto campgrounds and a seasonal ranger station. Though the Forest Service hopes to build a bypass around the washout, environmental concerns and a sagging economy have slowed the effort.

But the road that remains is a great getaway as it climbs west out of Brinnon and through farmland where, after a short **1.0** mile, you'll pass an "Elk Crossing" sign. Keep a lookout here, because a herd of the big animals has taken up residence in the lower valley. At **1.7** miles, pass a junction with Appaloosa Road and head down to river level at **3.2** miles. The road winds past big farms and summer homes for about 4.0 miles before the pavement ends and the byway gains its Forest Service designation, 2610.

The Dosewallips River Road parallels the river for several miles.

You'll drive through a forest of alder and big firs, both at riverside and several hundred yards from the rushing Dosewallips. At **9.2** miles, you'll pass what was once the Steelhead Campground on the left and in another 0.1 mile, arrive at the overgrown Tunnel Creek trailhead on the right. The Tunnel Creek Trail is one of the steepest in the forest, rivaled only by the Lake Constance way trail in Olympic National Park.

Beyond, the road climbs away from the river to cross Gamm Creek, which occasionally carves its own impassable canyon in the road. Next, you'll drop back to forest along the river, pass a couple of "diverse" campsites in the forest by the river, and arrive at **10.1** miles and the washout. To get an idea of the power of the Dosewallips River, walk the short distance to the edge of the road and look more than a 100 yards upstream to the west end of the washout.

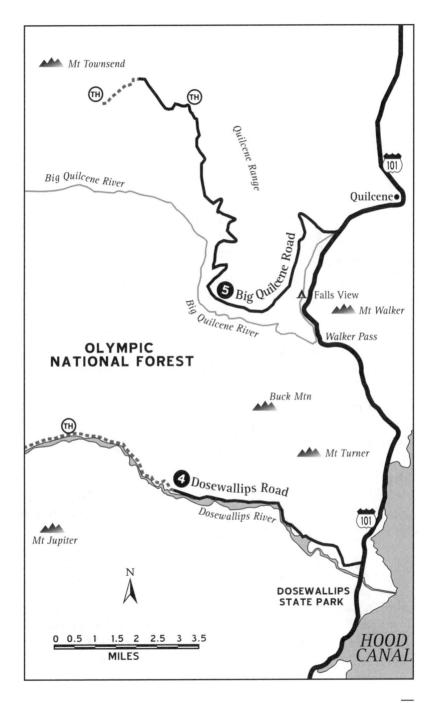

5. Big Quilcene Road

RATING	⊛⊛⊛
DISTANCE	16.4 miles
ROAD SURFACE	Paved/Graded gravel
ROAD CONDITION	Good
ROAD GRADE	Steep
PUCKER FACTOR	Sightseeing OK
ACCESSIBLE	Summer, fall
LAND MANAGER/CONTACT	Olympic National Forest, Hood Canal Ranger District, (360) 765-2200, www.fs.fed.us/r6/olympic
TRAILHEADS	Notch Pass, Lower and Upper Mount Townsend
NOTES	Northwest Forest Pass ($5 daily, $30 annually) required at trailheads

The Drive

The young forest above the Quilcene River gives the road an alpine feel and sightseers the opportunity to spot deer, black bear, and elk on hillsides above and below the byway.

Getting There

From Highway 101 in Quilcene, follow Highway 101 south past the Hood Canal Ranger District office for 1.3 miles to the Penny Creek Road and turn right. (See map on page 13.) GPS location: N47°49.019'; W122°54.237'

The Road

Though it's called the Big Quilcene River Road, Forest Road 27 seldom provides a glimpse of the river as it races through a narrow canyon in the woods below the road. That's no reason to complain, because the views of the mountains above and the chance at spotting wildlife at just about every turn of this winding one-lane thoroughfare are cause enough to take this Sunday drive.

Follow the Penny Creek Road for **1.4** miles, where the pavement ends—for a short, bumpy stretch—and turn left. A sign here gives mileages to various trailheads, including the Big Quilcene Trail, Tunnel Creek, and Mount Townsend. You'll climb up through a clear-cut and at **3.5** miles, cross into the Olympic National Forest, where the pavement begins. From here, the road is single-lane with paved turnouts.

Snow lingers on the upper Big Quilcene Road.

At **4.7** miles, you'll pass a junction with the forest road leading to the Tunnel Creek trailhead. Keep right and follow the Big Quilcene Road as it continues to climb above the river valley to a junction with the road leading to the Lower Big Quilcene trailhead. Stay right and at **6.3** miles, pass a "diverse" campsite on the left. Those who don't wish to purchase a Northwest Forest Pass will find diverse sites such as this the best places to legally park.

Next, **7.1** miles from Highway 101, pass a junction with Forest Road 27-090 and in another 0.4 mile, Forest Road 27-100. The Notch Pass Trail crosses the road at **9.3** miles and you'll keep left 1.0 mile beyond at a junction with Forest Road 27-140. Forested peaks surround you now, high above the Big Quilcene River. At **11.2** miles, stay right at a junction with Forest Road 2750, which leads to the upper Big Quilcene River trailhead, a favorite with mountain bike riders who can ride the single track downstream to the lower trailhead.

At mile **14.3**, find Forest Road 2760, which leads to the lower Mount Townsend trailhead. Keep right and continue climbing for another 1.3 miles to a junction with Forest Road 27-190, which leads in a short 1.0 mile to the Upper Mount Townsend trailhead. The pavement ends here, and you'll turn left on this rugged, cliffside road and drive to the upper trailhead. Though the road continues past the parking area, it grows increasingly rough and overgrown, so the trailhead is your turnaround point.

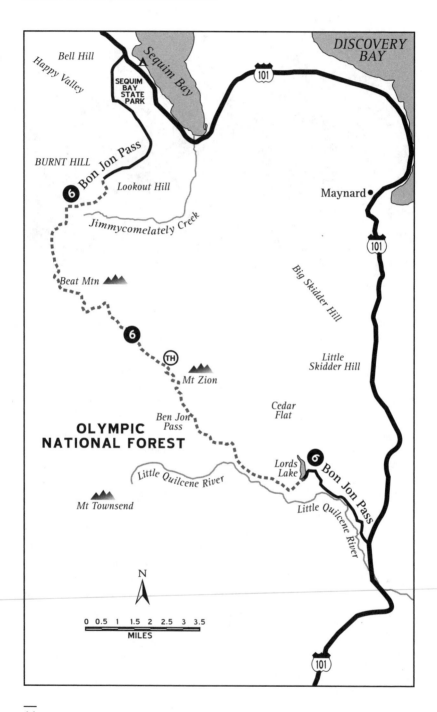

6. Bon Jon Pass

RATING	❀❀
DISTANCE	27.5 miles
ROAD SURFACE	Paved/Graded gravel
ROAD CONDITION	Good
ROAD GRADE	Steep
PUCKER FACTOR	Sightseeing OK
ACCESSIBLE	Spring–fall
LAND MANAGER/CONTACT	Olympic National Forest, Hood Canal Ranger District, (360) 765-2200, www.fs.fed.us/r6/olympic
TRAILHEADS	Mount Zion
NOTES	Northwest Forest Pass ($5 daily, $30 annually) required at trailheads

The Drive

Sunday drivers looking for a byway that climbs from lowland forest to mountainside views on the dry side of the Olympic Mountains will like this road.

Getting There

From Highway 101 in Quilcene, drive north for 1.9 miles to the Lords Lake Loop Road and turn left. GPS location: N47°50.357'; W122°53.364'

The Road

The road up and over Bon Jon Pass and past the Mount Zion trailhead is a pleasant way to cross part of the Olympic Mountains without driving around them on Highway 101. It's a scenic, forested alternative to the busy highway, one where you'll want to slow down and enjoy the view and watch for wildlife.

Follow Lords Lake Loop Road for **3.7** miles to a junction with the road leading to Bon Jon Pass, Forest Road 28, where the pavement ends. Turn left to drive along Lords Lake, a water reservoir for the Quilcene community. The lake is mostly hidden by timber, and a high fence keeps people and animals out. The water is pewter on a cloudy day and stretches north into the fog, where firs are silhouetted on a tiny island.

The road enters Olympic National Forest at **4.3** miles, and you'll stay right on Forest Road 28, climbing in deep forest above the Little Quilcene River. The thoroughfare reaches a junction **7.9** miles from Highway 101 where Forest Road 27 joins FR 28, and you'll bear right around the hairpin and begin

Fog lifts from a meadow near the top of Bon Jon Pass.

climbing toward Bon Jon Pass. At mile **8.8**, the road gets steeper and climbs above a meadow where a tributary to the Little Quilcene River is born. Reach 2,960-foot Bon Jon 0.5 mile beyond, where there's a junction with a forest road leading to the Little Quilcene Trail. Keep right and continue climbing on FR 28 to the Mount Zion trailhead, a good picnic stop if you've got a Northwest Forest Pass, **11.4** miles from Highway 101.

The road now crosses into the Dungeness and Gold Creek watersheds, and you can look west across the valley to the steep rock faces above the Dungeness River. Stay left at **12.2** miles and right at **12.7** miles. Your drive continues along FR 28, passing junctions at **13.7** and **15.3** miles. Follow FR 28 to the left at the junction with Forest Road 2840 and at **19.5** miles, pass a junction with Forest Road 2880 on the left, which drops to the Dungeness Forks Campground about 2 miles down.

Just beyond, the road leaves Olympic National Forest and pavement begins as the road becomes the Palo Alto Road. It passes several farms, takes a sharp turn to the east, and drops down to Highway 101 just east of Sequim. Seattle-bound drivers can turn right at the Louella Road, mile **25.3**, which cuts down to Highway 101 at Sequim Bay State Park. Visibility for motorists turning south onto Highway 101 is better at this junction.

7. Deer Park Road

RATING	⊕⊕⊕⊕⊕
DISTANCE	17.2 miles
ROAD SURFACE	Paved/Graded dirt
ROAD CONDITION	Good
ROAD GRADE	Extremely steep
PUCKER FACTOR	White knuckles
ACCESSIBLE	Summer, fall
LAND MANAGER/CONTACT	Olympic National Park, (360) 565-3130, www.nps.gov/olym
TRAILHEADS	Obstruction Point, Three Forks, Slide Camp
CAMPGROUNDS	Deer Park
NOTES	Narrow, steep winding road; not recommended for trailers or big recreational vehicles

The Drive

This is one of the premier mountain roads in the state, climbing almost a mile into the Olympic Mountains and one of the nicest auto-accessible tent campgrounds anywhere.

Getting There

From Highway 101 just east of Port Angeles and the Morse Creek valley, turn left onto the Deer Park Road just east of the Deer Park Cinema and auto dealership. GPS location: N48°06.343'; W123°20.732'

The Road

You can see Blue Mountain, where you're headed, from Highway 101 almost before you get to Sequim. It's a broad, snowy peak that guards the interior Olympic Mountains and nurses the Dungeness and Gray Wolf Rivers. The mountain is 6,007 feet high and the road reaches a spot just 700 feet below the summit. The campground looks across the valleys of the Cameron and Grand Creeks to the rugged Needles and Gray Wolf range.

The drive begins on a paved road that climbs gently past residences and farms along the east rim of the Morse Creek valley. The road turns to gravel and dirt past the Township Line Road and climbs into a high farmland valley before entering Olympic National Park **9.1** miles from Highway 101. The road is gated here in the winter when snow begins to build up, and it doesn't reopen until it thaws, usually by mid-July.

The Needles from Deer Park.

You'll begin climbing more steeply just beyond the gate and round two switchbacks to gain elevation. The road is wide enough to allow two-way traffic, but there's little room to spare. You'll find a number of wide turnouts along the way. Once past the switchbacks, the road climbs to a narrow viewpoint overlooking the forest and valley below, about **12.5** miles from Highway 101. Here the road turns sharply to the east and gets steeper, gobbling up huge chunks of elevation as it heads toward the north ridge of Blue Mountain. The view to the south and west is precipitous as the mountainside dives into the valley below.

The road turns south underneath the face of Blue Mountain and begins a final twisting climb to timberline and the steep open meadows below Deer Park, **16.0** miles from the highway. In another 0.5 mile, you'll find a junction with a road that drops steeply to a seasonal ranger station on the west shoulder of Blue Mountain. A trail here follows an abandoned road toward Obstruction Point (drive #9). Just beyond the junction, the view to the south opens like a mountain portfolio. At mile **16.5**, the road from the ranger stations rejoins the thoroughfare and continues to one of two campground loops. Another road branches to the left for about 100 yards to a trailhead parking area, where routes down two Three Forks and Slide Camp begin.

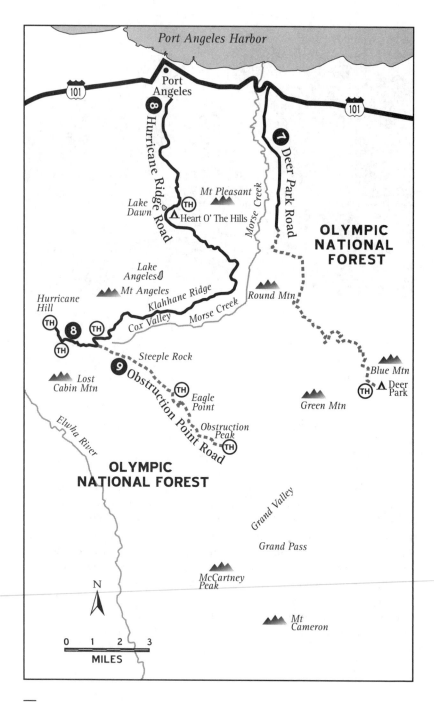

Port Angeles Harbor

101

Port
Angeles

8

101

Hurricane Ridge Road

7 Deer Park Road

Mt Pleasant

Morse Creek

TH

Lake
Dawn

Heart O' The Hills

OLYMPIC
NATIONAL
FOREST

Lake
Angeles

Mt Angeles

Klahhane Ridge

Round Mtn

Hurricane
Hill

Cox Valley

Morse Creek

TH

8

TH

TH

9 Obstruction Point Road

Steeple Rock

Blue Mtn

Lost
Cabin Mtn

TH

Eagle
Point

TH

Deer
Park

Green Mtn

Obstruction
Peak

TH

Elwha River

OLYMPIC
NATIONAL FOREST

Grand Valley

Grand Pass

N

McCartney
Peak

Mt
Cameron

0   1   2   3
MILES

8. Hurricane Ridge Road

RATING	✹✹✹✹✹
DISTANCE	19.3 miles
ROAD SURFACE	Paved
ROAD CONDITION	Excellent
ROAD GRADE	Steep
PUCKER FACTOR	Sightseeing OK
ACCESSIBLE	Year-round
LAND MANAGER/CONTACT	Olympic National Park, (360) 565-3130, www.nps.gov/olym
TRAILHEADS	Lake Creek, Heather Park, Lake Angeles, Switchback, Hurricane Nature, Klahhane Ridge, Wolf Creek, Hurricane Hill
CAMPGROUNDS	Heart o' the Hills
NOTES	Entry fee ($15/7-day, $30 annually) required. Watch for deer on road.

The Drive

This is one of the tamer wild roads in this guide, a beautiful drive to a mountaintop meadow, wildflower haven, and views that include Vancouver Island across the Strait of Juan de Fuca.

Getting There

From Highway 101 in Port Angeles, turn south on Race Street and drive to the Olympic National Park Visitor Center on the right. The Hurricane Ridge Road begins just past the visitor center with a right turn. (See map on page 22.) GPS location: N48°05.915'; W123°25.517'

The Road

You can't beat this road for views and almost certain encounters with black-tailed deer and Canada jays that mug tourists for handouts (don't feed the wildlife!). Now, thanks largely to donations from Port Angeles residents, city and county commissioners, and Olympic National Park, the road is open daily and maintained throughout the winter, giving snowshoers and downhill and cross-country skiers and snowboarders a place to play.

The road follows a narrow forest corridor from the city, climbing gently at first toward the rocky Olympic crags hunched above Port Angeles like lurking trolls. You'll climb in **3.0** miles to an overlook of the lower Morse Creek valley and Mount Pleasant, negotiate a couple of sharp curves, and,

The Hurricane Ridge Road climbs underneath Klahhane Ridge on its way to the Hurricane Visitor Center.

just beyond a junction with the Lake Dawn Road on the right, arrive at the Heart o' the Hills entrance station. Here, **5.2** miles from the visitor center, you'll be asked to pay a $15 per carload entry fee, good for seven consecutive days.

The Heart o' the Hills Campground is just past the entrance station on the left, and the road begins to climb more steeply in old-growth forest, winding along the hillside. The view to the east begins to open up as you round ridges above the Morse Creek valley, and at mile **9.1**, you can pull out to a viewpoint that looks down on Port Angeles, across the strait to Vancouver Island, and east to Sequim and the Dungeness Spit.

Beyond, you'll round a corner and enter the first of three short tunnels, emerging from the last tunnel to a far different view to the south. The forest here is more open and sunny, and you can look across the Morse Creek valley to the east and see the angled rocky slash of the Deer Park Road (drive #7). The road continues its upward pace, twisting along the steep hillside and eventually making a sharp turn to the right to a switchback corner, **14.9** miles from the visitor center. The Switchback Trail begins at this corner, a steep pathway that climbs to the bald Klahhane Ridge, just north of Mount Angeles. Round a few more corners and climb another 3.0 miles, now in open alpine meadows, to a final corner where again, the view changes to a startling panorama of mountains, twisting and scratching the clouds from east to west to south. No matter how many times you round this corner, the vista will always catch you by surprise. Shortly after, you'll climb into the parking area at the Hurricane Ridge Visitor Center, **17.8** miles up the road. The Obstruction Point Road (drive #9) begins here, but you can continue past the Hurricane Ridge Visitor Center for almost 2.0 miles to a picnic area with views of Mount Olympus, the highest peak in the Olympic range at 7,965 feet, and a paved nature trail leading to the site of a World War II aircraft spotter's cabin atop Hurricane Hill.

9. Obstruction Point Road

RATING	⚙⚙⚙⚙⚙
DISTANCE	7.7 miles
ROAD SURFACE	Graded dirt
ROAD CONDITION	Good
ROAD GRADE	Steep
PUCKER FACTOR	White knuckles
ACCESSIBLE	Midsummer, fall
LAND MANAGER/CONTACT	Olympic National Park, (360) 565-3130, www.nps.gov/olym
TRAILHEADS	P. J. Lake, Obstruction Point, Grand Valley, Grand Lake
NOTES	Entry fee ($15/7-day, $30 annually) required. Dusty in summer.

The Drive

One of the highest roads on the Olympic Peninsula takes you through forests and alpine meadows to vistas of mountains and wilderness river valleys.

Getting There

Follow Highway 101 to Port Angeles and turn left on Race Street. Follow Race Street past the Olympic National Park Visitor Center (restrooms, visitor information) and turn right on the Hurricane Ridge Road, which climbs from sea level to 5,240 feet in about 17 miles. Drive 5.2 miles to the Olympic National Park entrance station, where you will be asked to pay the entry fee.

Continue on the paved Hurricane Ridge Road about 12 miles to the Hurricane Ridge Visitor Center (restrooms, snack bar, visitor information) and the Hurricane Ridge parking area. The beginning of the Obstruction Point Road is on the left, at the north end of the parking lot, and requires a U-turn or turnaround at the parking area. (See map on page 22.) GPS location: N47°58.178'; W123°58.631'

The Road

From the very beginning, this lane declares itself a mountain thoroughfare in no uncertain terms, dropping steeply down the side of an alpine meadow. The scenery tumbles off the road on the passenger side to the Lillian and Elwha River valleys, and beyond to the interior peaks of Olympic National Park, including Mount Olympus, the highest in the park at 7,965 feet.

Heavy snows kept the Obstruction Point Road closed until August 2011.

After **0.6** mile, the road levels off and rides the crest of a ridge through a corridor of pungent fir and sloping meadows filled with summer wildflowers where Columbia black-tailed deer can often be seen. Drive another **0.8** mile to two short hairpin turns that lead across the crest of a ridge, with views to the north of the Strait of Juan de Fuca and the snowcapped peaks of the Olympics to the south and west.

Beyond, the road begins a steep sidehill climb toward Steeple Rock, the sharp, rocky pinnacle off the driver's side. This rock, about **2.0** miles from Hurricane Ridge, is a popular practice area for rock climbers and a snow-shoeing destination in the winter. You'll see a bare knoll off the passenger side below Steeple Road where a helicopter can land. I know this because one landed there to evacuate me, a victim of hypothermia, on Super Bowl Sunday many, many years ago.

Past Steeple Rock, the road traverses the sidehill and levels off just below the ridgecrest, then turns north at **2.9** miles. This section of the road might interest a geologist; the forest and meadows to the right represent a "sag," or portion of the ridge, which settled below the main ridge on the left.

At **3.2** miles, you'll arrive at the Waterhole Picnic Area, a flat, forested glade that offers shade and shelter on hot summer days. A trail on the driver's side of the road leads 1.0 very steep mile down—and up—to tiny P. J. Lake. This is one of the lakes Olympic National Park officials are trying to rid of nonnative eastern brook trout, so there is no limit on the number of fish you can catch. The trail to the lake is extremely steep, however, and shouldn't be attempted by anyone who isn't in good physical condition.

Past Waterhole, the road begins a steep climb to 6,247-foot-high Eagle Point, switching back twice. These two switchbacks are usually the last spots to clear of snowdrifts and sometimes keep the road closed until mid-July. The road here is also usually in the worst condition at this point.

Beyond Eagle Point, you'll find yourself on a wide, rolling meadow that is the northern roof of the Olympic Mountains. You can look down on the Lillian River valley to the southwest and across the Strait of Juan de Fuca to Vancouver Island to the north. Use caution and go slowly as the road, which seems to drop straight down to a saddle, actually rounds a hidden turn. A pullout at the saddle is a good spot to take in the view, about 7.4 miles from Hurricane Ridge.

From here, the road begins a final climb through alpine forest to the parking area and end of the road below 6,450-foot-high Obstruction Point. There's an outhouse at Obstruction Point and a broad meadow that holds snow well into July, where marmots cool themselves on hot days.

Two hiking trails head into the park wilderness from the parking area. A trail crosses the meadow to the north, climbing and eventually dropping in about 4.0 miles to Moose and Grand Lakes. A second trail begins at the end of the road, crossing the headwall of Grand Valley and following the crest of the ridge to Deer Park, about 8.0 miles to the northeast. This was the proposed route of Obstruction Point Road, a Civilian Conservation Corps project that came to a halt with World War II.

A final note: In the fall, try to avoid returning in the evening. You drive directly into the setting sun on the steep, final hill back to the Hurricane Ridge parking lot. Visibility is all but nil.

10. Oil City Road

RATING	✇
DISTANCE	10.7 miles
ROAD SURFACE	Paved/Graded dirt
ROAD CONDITION	Fair
ROAD GRADE	Moderate
PUCKER FACTOR	Flatlanders welcome
ACCESSIBLE	Year-round
LAND MANAGER/CONTACT	Olympic National Park, (360) 565-3130, www.nps.gov/olym
TRAILHEADS	Oil City
CAMPGROUNDS	Cottonwood
NOTES	Muddy and rough road beginning at park boundary

The Drive

This road takes you on a tour through clear-cuts and logged-over land to protected rainforest in Olympic National Park. A short trail at the end of the road leads to a lonely Pacific Ocean beach.

Getting There

From Forks, drive about 14 miles south on Highway 101 to its junction with the Oil City Road and turn right. GPS location: N47°48.563'; W124°15.481'

The Road

I chose this road after misreading a map, thinking the road actually ended at an Olympic National Park beach north of the mouth of the Hoh River. Actually, the road ends at a park trailhead 0.7 mile short of the beach. I considered not including the Oil City Road here, but decided it would make a good field trip for motorists interested in seeing the contrast between logged clear-cuts and old-growth forest. Here you'll see a bit of both, and if you're up for a short walk, visit a sandy Pacific Ocean beach where you can walk for more than a mile.

The road begins with a short downhill section to a one-lane gravel road that negotiates a 0.2-mile route that appears to be the victim of a washout from the barren hillside above. You'll be back on paved road **0.5** mile from the highway junction and cruise through thick new-growth forest on your left for 2.4 miles to a junction with a road leading down to the Cottonwood Campground on the banks of the Hoh River. The campground and

The Hoh River rolls toward the Pacific at a viewpoint on the Oil City Road.

boat launch and takeout are managed by the state Department of Natural Resources, and you'll need a Discover Pass ($10 daily, $30–$35 annually) if you plan to park there.

Beyond the junction, the road alternately passes sections of new forest and clear-cuts where there's little evidence of reforestation. The pavement ends **5.2** miles from the highway and 4.0 miles later, drops to river level and passes several private houses. You'll arrive at the Olympic National Park boundary **10.5** miles from Highway 101, and the scenery changes dramatically. The Hoh River rolls toward the ocean and big cedars stretch toward the sky.

You can drive another 0.2 mile to the Oil City trailhead, where there's a restroom and Olympic National Park kiosk. The trail leads west in old forest beside the Hoh River and can get muddy and slippery in places on the all-too-frequent rainy days. But the ocean beach that stretches north for about 1.5 miles is a great place to get away from it all.

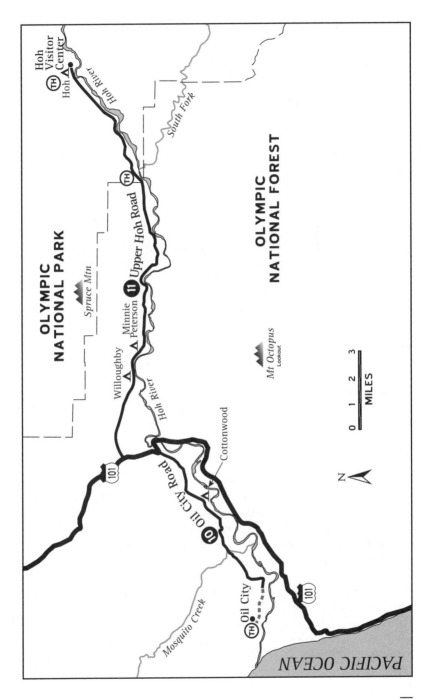

11. Upper Hoh Road

RATING	⚙⚙⚙
DISTANCE	18.5 miles
ROAD SURFACE	Paved
ROAD CONDITION	Good
ROAD GRADE	Flat
PUCKER FACTOR	Flatlanders welcome
ACCESSIBLE	Year-round
LAND MANAGER/CONTACT	Olympic National Park, (360) 565-3130, www.nps.gov/olym
TRAILHEADS	Hoh-Bogachiel, Hoh Nature, Hoh River
CAMPGROUNDS	Willoughby Creek, Minnie Peterson, Hoh River
NOTES	Entry fee ($15/7-day, $30 annually) required. Watch for deer and elk on road.

The Drive

The road to the Hoh Rain Forest Visitor Center in Olympic National Park is a must-do for any motorist heading to the ocean on Highway 101.

Getting There

From Forks, follow Highway 101 for 13.0 miles south to the junction with the Upper Hoh Road and turn left. (See map on page 31.) GPS location: N47°49.541'; W124°15.809'

The Road

This well-traveled thoroughfare passes historic private farms, state Department of Natural Resources forestland and campgrounds, and Olympic National Forest before ending at a campground and visitor center in Olympic National Park. Two short nature trails begin at the center, as does a 17.0-mile trail that climbs to the Blue Glacier on Mount Olympus, the highest peak in the Olympic Mountains.

The road winds down in the first **1.0** mile, crossing Hell Roaring Creek and traversing logged timberlands where, on clear days, you can look east toward snowcapped Olympic peaks. At **3.7** miles, you'll arrive at Willoughby Creek Campground, managed by the state Department of Natural Resources. You'll need a Discover Pass ($10 daily, $30–$35 annually) to picnic here, and there are a couple of nice riverside spots for camping and Hoh River–watching.

The Upper Hoh Road passes a campground named for Olympic wrangler Minnie Peterson on its way to Olympic National Park.

In another 1.4 miles, arrive at the Minnie Peterson Campground, another Department of Natural Resources–managed facility where a Discover Pass is required if you plan to stay. The campground is named for a hardy Olympic Peninsula pioneer woman who led horse-packing trips in the Olympic Mountains for more than a half century. She was around 80 years old when she guided her last trip into the mountains, and she died in 1989 at the age of 90. You'll pass the Peterson family farm farther along the road.

The road narrows as it enters Olympic National Park, **12.5** miles from its junction with Highway 101. The forest here is much the same as it was when white settlers first arrived on American shores, and some of the cedars, Sitka spruce—you'll see a huge example just off the park road—and Douglas fir were already pushing skyward then. The road winds through this ancient forest, where deer, elk, and black bears can often be seen, to a park entrance booth, where you'll be asked to pay the entry fee. Beyond, the road passes the entrance to the Olympic National Park Hoh River Campground and ends in a large parking area at the Hoh Rain Forest Visitor Center, **18.5** miles from the highway.

The visitor center is filled with interpretive displays and an information desk where friendly park rangers can answer all of your questions. Two short nature trails begin just outside, taking visitors on loop trips through the moss-draped forest. Keep a sharp eye out for elk along the trails; a herd often wanders the forest and even the campground here.

12. Lake Quinault Loop

RATING	⚙⚙⚙
DISTANCE	28.4 miles
ROAD SURFACE	Paved/Graded gravel
ROAD CONDITION	Good
ROAD GRADE	Flat
PUCKER FACTOR	Flatlanders welcome
ACCESSIBLE	Year-round
LAND MANAGER/CONTACT	Olympic National Forest, Pacific Ranger District, Quinault Office, (360) 288-2525, www.fs.fed.us/r6/olympic; Olympic National Park, Quinault Ranger Station, (360) 288-2444, www.nps.gov/olym
TRAILHEADS	Fletcher Canyon, Colonel Bob, Wright Canyon, Willaby Creek, Big Tree Grove
CAMPGROUNDS	Gatton Creek, Falls Creek, Willaby
NOTES	Northwest Forest Pass ($5 daily, $30 annually) required at Olympic National Forest picnic areas

The Drive
The ride around this beautiful lake takes you through deep forest and past mountain views to a splendid old lakeside lodge in Olympic National Park.

Getting There
Turn east off Highway 101 onto the North Shore Road, just north of the community of Amanda Park at the west end of Lake Quinault. GPS location: N47°28,149'; W123°55.409'

The Road
The Quinault River rolls into Lake Quinault, born of the snows and Quinault Glacier on Mount Anderson and the rugged mountains that ring the Low Divide in Olympic National Park. The lake is clear and cold, and the Quinault River empties into the Pacific Ocean at Taholah on the Quinault Indian Reservation.

The road around the lake and up the Quinault River is mostly paved and makes a good Sunday drive for those visiting Kalaloch on the Pacific Ocean or staying at the historic Lake Quinault Lodge. Begin by driving above the lake's north shore for **3.7** miles to the July Creek Picnic Area, which is managed by

Thimbleberry grows along the North Shore Road where the Quinault River rolls into Lake Quinault.

Olympic National Park. You'll find a trail leading down to tables with views across the water, where July Creek tumbles into the lake.

Beyond, the road enters a wide plain and passes the Olympic National Park Quinault Ranger Station, **5.9** miles from Highway 101. You'll cross a one-lane bridge at **7.0** miles and find the beginning of a 5.0-mile section of gravel road **8.3** miles from the highway. Shortly after you're back on paved road, you'll arrive at a junction with the South Shore Road, **14.6** miles from the highway.

For a 6.0-mile side trip, follow the road leading to the North Fork Ranger Station in Olympic National Park. In addition to the seasonal ranger station, you'll pass a trail leading a short 1.0 mile to Irely Lake and the North Fork Campground, a primitive car-camping facility on the Quinault River.

Back on the South Shore Road, you'll cross the Quinault River on a bridge that provides good views upstream to the Quinault Valley and, on a clear day, the mountains above. Turn right just across the bridge and take the gravel South Shore Road as it follows the river downstream past the Fletcher Canyon trailhead, **16.3** miles from Highway 101. You'll get back on paved road at the Grays Harbor County line, **20.0** miles from the highway.

Pass a nice waterfall 1.5 miles beyond, and slow down to pass the community of Quinault, **24.7** miles from the beginning of your drive. You'll find a grocery store, motel, and restaurant. Just down the road, at **25.3** miles, pass Gatton Creek Campground and in another 0.5 mile, Falls Creek Campground, both managed by Olympic National Forest.

At mile **25.9**, you'll arrive at the Lake Quinault Lodge, a splendid old building built in 1926, now operated by an Olympic National Park concessionaire. It's a favorite of tourists who hike some of the nearby trails or rent canoes to paddle on the lake. Farther down the road, you'll pass the best Olympic National Forest campground on the lake, Willaby, at **26.5** miles. Another 0.25 mile beyond, a short nature trail climbs into the forest above the lake.

At **27.1** miles, you'll find a junction with the Amanda Park Road. If you're headed south on Highway 101 toward Aberdeen and Hoquiam, turn left here. Stay right if you're northbound on Highway 101, reaching Amanda Park and the junction with Highway 101 at **28.4** miles.

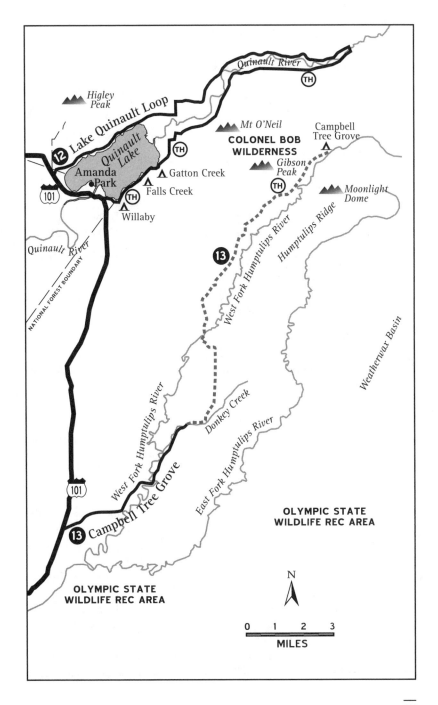

13. Campbell Tree Grove

RATING	⊛⊛⊛
DISTANCE	23.3 miles
ROAD SURFACE	Paved/Graded gravel
ROAD CONDITION	Good
ROAD GRADE	Moderate
PUCKER FACTOR	Flatlanders welcome
ACCESSIBLE	Year-round
LAND MANAGER/CONTACT	Olympic National Forest, Pacific Ranger District, Quinault Office, (360) 288-2525, www.fs.fed.us/r6/olympic
TRAILHEADS	Pete's Creek
CAMPGROUNDS	Campbell Tree Grove
NOTES	Northwest Forest Pass ($5 daily, $30 annually) required

The Drive

The road to Campbell Tree Grove Campground passes through fir and cedar forest, both old and new, to a riverside campground surrounded by 600-year-old evergreens.

Getting There

From Highway 101 at Amanda Park, drive 14.2 miles south to the Donkey Creek Road, Forest Road 22, and turn left. (See map on page 37.) GPS location: N47°16.030'; W123°55.091'

The Road

The Campbell Tree Grove is one of the least visited spots in the Pacific rain forest, and that is both a blessing and a bane. It's unfortunate, because the grove and its campground are among the prettiest in Olympic National Forest. And it's great, because at times you'll have this quiet spot by the West Fork of the Humptulips River all to yourself.

The area is popular with bird-watchers, who often practice "birding by ear"—camping overnight and listening to the calls of birds they often don't see. Marbled Murrelets nest in the mighty cedar and fir, and Northern Pygmy Owls, Pacific-slope Flycatchers, two thrush species, chickadees, and winter wrens are usually heard but not seen.

The paved road begins with a turn to the north, traversing mostly refor-ested areas and alder thickets. You'll get distant views of the western Olympic

The parking area for visitors is just across from Campbell Tree Grove Campsite No. 1.

Mountains through the trees. Stay on the Donkey Creek Road for **8.2** miles to Forest Road 2204 and turn left, passing the Humptulips Work Center. The road narrows and the pavement ends at **11.2** miles, still in mostly second-growth forest.

You'll arrive at a Y intersection at **12.4** miles and bear right, passing the Pete's Creek trailhead **19.2** miles from Highway 101. This steep trail climbs to the summit of Colonel Bob, the 4,492-foot site of an old fire lookout. The peak, and the surrounding Colonel Bob Wilderness in Olympic National

Forest, is named for Robert G. Ingersoll, a Union Army colonel who fought at Shiloh.

Past the trailhead, you'll climb a rounded hill before dropping into the river flats and the ancient forest along the West Fork of the Humptulips River, arriving at the Campbell Tree Grove Campground entrance **23.2** miles from the highway. Turn right at the campground and find parking adjacent to Campsite No. 1. The primitive campground has 11 sites, and camping among the giant evergreens by the river is free.

14. Green Mountain Road

RATING	✪
DISTANCE	4.1 miles
ROAD SURFACE	Graded gravel
ROAD CONDITION	Good
ROAD GRADE	Steep
PUCKER FACTOR	Flatlanders welcome
ACCESSIBLE	Summer
LAND MANAGER/CONTACT	Washington Department of Natural Resources, South Puget Sound Region, (360) 825-1631, www.dnr.wa.gov
TRAILHEADS	Beaver Pond, Horse Camp
CAMPGROUNDS	Horse Camp
NOTES	Discover Pass ($10 daily, $30–$35 annually) required

The Drive

This gated road climbs to a great view of the Olympic Mountains to the west and the entire Puget Sound region to the east. The road is open on summer weekends.

Getting There

Follow Highway 3 north from Bremerton to the Newberry Hill Road exit and turn left on the Newberry Hill Road, following it 3.1 miles west to the Seabeck Highway. Turn left on the Seabeck Highway and drive 2 miles to the Holly Road. Turn right on the Holly Road and drive 4.2 miles to the Lake Tahuya Road and turn left. Drive 1 mile to the Green Mountain Road, GM-1, on the left. GPS location: N47°34.845'; W122°50.087'

The Road

The Green Mountain Road is usually open weekends from Memorial Day to Labor Day, popular with motorists headed for one of the highest mountains on the Kitsap Peninsula at 1,639 feet. Green Mountain State Forest is a working forest, meaning you're likely to see areas in the woods that have been logged or marked for future logging.

You'll drive east for **0.8** mile before turning downhill and crossing Tin Mine Creek, then climbing a steep hill, switching back at **1.1** miles, and passing a marshy area on your left. The road continues to climb and at **2.7** miles, joins a road that leads to the Green Mountain Horse Camp. Stay right and

The Brothers in the Olympic Mountains shine from a viewpoint on the way up the Green Mountain Road.

round a sharp switchback, climbing to a good view to the west of the Olympic Mountains, **3.0** miles from the Lake Tahuya Road.

Beyond, the road turns south and begins a steep climb to a wide parking lot with picnic tables and a restroom, **4.1** miles from the beginning. A steep, rocky trail leads from the west end of the parking area for about 0.4 mile to the Green Mountain Vista at the summit of the peak, where the views are best.

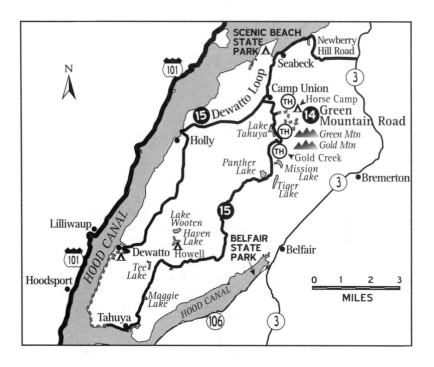

15. Dewatto Loop

RATING	✪✪✪
DISTANCE	75.4 miles
ROAD SURFACE	Paved/Graded gravel
ROAD CONDITION	Fair
ROAD GRADE	Steep
PUCKER FACTOR	Sightseeing OK
ACCESSIBLE	Year-round
LAND MANAGER/CONTACT	Washington Department of Natural Resources, South Puget Sound Region, (360) 825-1631, www.dnr.wa.gov
TRAILHEADS	Gold Creek
CAMPGROUNDS	Scenic Beach, Howell Lake
NOTES	Discover Pass ($10 daily, $30–$35 annually) required. Muddy in fall and winter.

The Drive

This long loop trip takes you along the less-crowded eastern shore of Hood Canal, with some great views west to the Olympic Mountains.

Getting There

Follow Highway 3 north from Bremerton to the Newberry Hill Road exit and turn west on the Newberry Hill Road. (See map on page 43.) GPS location: N48°38.211'; W122°42.350'

The Road

Here's one of the longest drives in this guide, passing through farm and forestland, historic villages and logging camps. You'll see some wild, unpopulated country that is within 90 minutes of Seattle and find wooded shores and lakes for picnicking or watching wildlife. In May, the scenery turns pink from thousands of wild rhododendron blossoms.

Begin by heading uphill on the Newberry Hill Road **3.1** miles to the Seabeck Highway and turn right. The "highway" is actually a paved county road that winds downhill to the shores of Hood Canal. You'll arrive at the Big Beef Creek Bridge after driving **5.6** miles and if you're there in September, park on the wide shoulder to watch silver salmon acrobatics and bald eagles cruising for an easy meal. Though this part of the Hood Canal waterfront is lined with homes, deer are plentiful here and share the road with motorists.

The view from the Dewatto Loop includes Hood Canal and Mount Constance.

You'll arrive in Seabeck **7.7** miles from the starting point. This village, with its marina, cafe, general store, and retreat center, was once a thriving lumber mill. Just beyond Seabeck, a road leads to the right to Scenic Beach State Park, a good spot for picnicking or walking the rocky beach. Stay left and climb away from Hood Canal through farmland and alder forest, passing an intersection with the NW Holly Road on the left, at **11.3** miles. This is where you'll close the loop around the eastern shore of Hood Canal.

Continue past Crosby, an old logging community, on the renamed Seabeck-Holly Road and in about 5.0 miles, drop down a hill to the quiet Hood Canal shoreline community of Holly. The view west looks up the valley of the Hamma Hamma River, across the water. At **17.9** miles, turn left on the Dewatto Road W and drive south through young forest and logged land, crossing from Kitsap to Mason counties near the intersection with the W Bear Creek Road, mile **21.0**.

The drive continues past the intersection on the NE Dewatto-Holly Road, passing farms and pastureland and winding downhill to cross the Dewatto River at **26.0** miles. This quiet watercourse is popular with anglers in the fall, with its community campground and picnic shelter just off the road, at mile **27.7**. The road follows the river to its wide Hood Canal mouth at Dewatto

Bay, a spectacular canal and Olympic Mountain viewpoint. At mile **28.6,** turn left on the NE Dewatto Road and climb 0.2 mile to the Burma Road and turn right. The pavement ends here and the road alternately drops and climbs steeply under a forest canopy of alder and fir, crossing a number of streams that rush into Hood Canal. Best views of Hood Canal and the Olympics are at the several wide turnouts at the high points along the road.

You'll drive about 10.0 miles above the east shore of Hood Canal, about 100 vertical feet above the water on a steep hillside. Houses are sparse in this area, although a cooperative housing community has carved a number of homes into the hillside. Most of the land is privately owned on the water side of the road. Above the road, the bluffs rise about 340 feet to a wide plateau filled with small lakes and logged extensively. The Burma Road is usually open throughout the year, but can get muddy or be washed out from time to time in the winter. It rarely snows here, but if it does, save your Sunday drive for another day.

You'll reach Brown's Point at mile **37.2** and get back on paved road, arriving at the waterfront community of Tahuya after driving **39.0** miles. Turn left on the NE Belfair-Tahuya Road at **39.7** miles, passing the NE Tahuya River Road on the right in another 0.4 mile. Follow NE Belfair-Tahuya Road north as it passes the NE Dewatto Road and the NE Tahuya-Blacksmith Road, both on the left. This part of the drive is mostly in land checkered by state Department of Natural Resources forest and private homes. You'll pass a number of small lakes, including Collins and Howell Lakes, and the latter has a small campground and picnic area. At mile **49.8,** turn left onto the NE Elfendahl Pass Road and follow it about 6.0 miles north to the junction with the W Bear Creek Road, mile **55.9.** Turn right here and follow the W Bear Creek Road past Panther Lake to the Gold Creek Road at mile **58.0.**

Turn left onto Gold Creek Road and drive 3.0 miles, passing the Department of Natural Resources Gold Creek trailhead, to Lake Tahuya. The road passes waterfront homes on this private lake and, at the northern end, turns west to join the Lake Tahuya Road at a Y intersection. Keep right and drive to an intersection with the NW Holly Road, **63.3** miles. Turn left to rejoin the Seabeck Highway and close the loop at **64.1** miles, passing Camp Union, a former logging camp, along the way.

To return to Highway 3, turn right on the Seabeck Highway and left on Newberry Hill Road.

MOUNT BAKER HIGHWAY

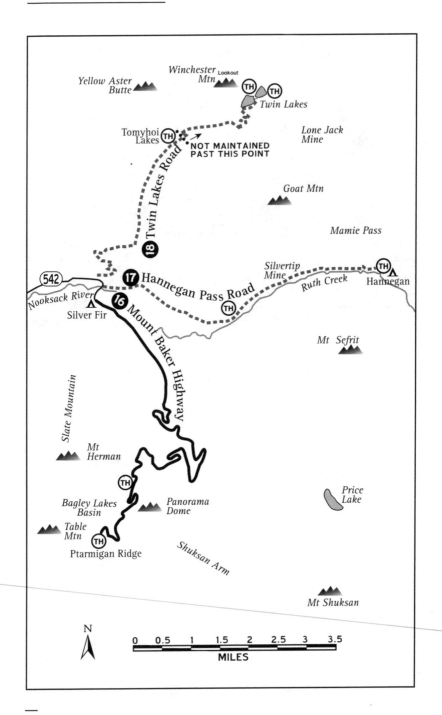

Yellow Aster Butte

Winchester Mtn Lookout

TH TH
Twin Lakes

Lone Jack Mine

Tomyhoi Lakes TH

NOT MAINTAINED PAST THIS POINT

Goat Mtn

18 Twin Lakes Road

Mamie Pass

Silvertip Mine

542

17 Hannegan Pass Road

Ruth Creek

TH Hannegan

Nooksack River

Silver Fir

16 Mount Baker Highway

TH

Mt Sefrit

Slate Mountain

Mt Herman

TH

Bagley Lakes Basin

Panorama Dome

Price Lake

Table Mtn

TH
Ptarmigan Ridge

Shuksan Arm

Mt Shuksan

N

0   0.5   1   1.5   2   2.5   3   3.5
MILES

16. Mount Baker Highway

RATING	⊗⊗⊗⊗
DISTANCE	10.2 miles
ROAD SURFACE	Paved
ROAD CONDITION	Excellent
ROAD GRADE	Steep
PUCKER FACTOR	Sightseeing OK
ACCESSIBLE	Year-round/summer only
LAND MANAGER/CONTACT	Mount Baker–Snoqualmie National Forest, Glacier Public Service Center, (360) 599-2714, www.fs.usda.gov/mbs
TRAILHEADS	Heather Meadows, Bagley Lakes, Lake Ann, Table Mountain, Ptarmigan Ridge
CAMPGROUNDS	Silver Fir
NOTES	Northwest Forest Pass ($5 daily, $30 annually) required

The Drive

The climb on this paved highway past the Mount Baker wintersports area ends at a mile-high viewpoint with vistas of two of the state's snow giants: Mount Baker and Mount Shuksan.

Getting There

From I-90 in Bellingham, take exit 255 to Highway 542 and drive east for about 46 miles to Silver Fir Campground just across the Nooksack River bridge. The drive to Artist Point on Highway 542 begins here. GPS location: N48°54.366'; W121°41.618'

The Road

This is one of the few high roads in this guide that is open year-round—at least until you get to the upper lodge of the Mount Baker wintersports area. In winter, the rest of the road is under as much as 30 to 40 feet of snow. The road above the wintersports area is usually free of snow by mid-July, although snowdrifts may linger beyond that time. In 2011, for example, snow was so deep that the road remained closed above Heather Meadows.

The road begins climbing immediately after crossing the Nooksack River and passing the entrance to Silver Fir Campground on the right. The campground makes a good car-camping base camp for visiting the high country

Artist Point, at the end of the Mount Baker Highway, affords this view of Mount Baker.

roads near Mount Baker's north side. You'll find riverside campsites under huge cedars and mountain hemlock trees.

The road takes a broad turn around a forested ridge where you can peek through the trees to the Nooksack River valley below and toward Hannegan Pass, at the head of the valley. Next, you'll pass a tumbling creek and waterfall, **1.6** miles from the startup. Water splashes off Mount Baker's snowfields throughout the summer and at **2.6** miles, you'll cross Bagley Creek, one of the larger tributaries to the Nooksack.

Take a sharp switchback at **2.9** miles and another at **3.3** miles from the beginning of your drive, snaking up the mountainside while surrounded by increasingly alpine forest. You'll cross another creek at **4.0** miles, then switchback at **4.9** miles, where a short side road leads to White Salmon Lodge. Look out for the splendid raven sculpture at the White Salmon gate, and if the lodge is open it's worth a visit simply to see the animal tracks cast into the floor. The lodge is a beautiful piece of architecture.

Beyond, you'll cross Razor Hone Creek at **5.4** miles, then climb the narrow Razor Hone canyon above, finally reaching beautiful alpine meadows **7.0** miles from your startup point. Heather Meadows, where pink and white heather cloaks the mountainside, cups two alpine tarns—Picture and Highwood Lakes—in a wildflower-ringed basin. Stay right at a junction with the downhill road at **7.7** miles and climb past the upper wintersports lodge to a picnic area and old rock shelter above the Bagley Lakes basin, on your right. A short road leads to the right to a parking area and the Bagley Lakes trailhead, **8.3** miles from your start.

The road continues to climb to Austin Pass, at **9.1** miles, before crossing a broad alpine basin, switching back, and climbing to a wide parking area at Artist Point. Views of 10,781-foot-high Mount Baker to the west, and Mount Shuksan, 9,131 feet high, to the east, dominate the scene. There's little need to leave the parking area for pictures, but if you'd like a walk, head out the Ptarmigan Ridge Trail for great views of the Baker Lake valley on the south side of the mountain.

17. Hannegan Pass Road

RATING	🎦🎦🎦🎦
DISTANCE	5.3 miles
ROAD SURFACE	Graded gravel
ROAD CONDITION	Fair
ROAD GRADE	Moderate
PUCKER FACTOR	Flatlanders welcome
ACCESSIBLE	Summer, fall
LAND MANAGER/CONTACT	Mount Baker–Snoqualmie National Forest, Glacier Public Service Center, (360) 599-2714, www.fs.usda.gov/mbs
TRAILHEADS	Goat Mountain, Hannegan Pass
CAMPGROUNDS	Silver Fir, Hannegan Trailhead
NOTES	Northwest Forest Pass ($5 daily, $30 annually) required

The Drive

Though short, the road to the Hannegan Pass trailhead is well worth the trip if you're traveling the Mount Baker Highway. Drive up the steep-walled valley on either side of Ruth Creek to see waterfalls and mountains above the creek.

Getting There

Follow Highway 542 for 13.3 miles east of the Glacier Public Service Center to the Hannegan Pass Road, Forest Road 32, and turn left. (See map on page 48.) GPS location: N48°54.366'; W121°41.618'

The Road

You don't get the feeling you're in the mountains at the start of this road, mostly because you're beside a rushing creek under a forest canopy. That won't last long, because you climb out of the forest to find mountains all around, and waterfalls cascading down from hanging snowfields above.

The road winds through a fir forest above the North Fork of the Nooksack River, which is bordered by tangled slide alder and evergreens. Drive **1.3** miles to a junction with Forest Road 34, which leads down to the North Fork of the Nooksack River. Keep left and begin climbing more steeply as the road enters the Ruth Creek valley. Goat Mountain, 6,820 feet high, scratches clouds on your left, and across the creek the north face of Nooksack Ridge

The road to Hannegan Pass begins near the Silver Fir Campground.

hoards snowfields well into summer, fueling the waterfalls off the mountainside. You'll pass a steep trail leading to Goat Mountain at **2.4** miles.

Beyond, the road continues to climb and the views open in subalpine country. Above, on the slopes of Goat Mountain, is one of the reasons this road exists: the old Silvertip Mine. Reach the end of the road at a primitive campground in **5.3** miles. Here you'll find an easy trail bordered by wildflowers in summer that climbs very gently for 0.6 mile to Donegan Creek, a good spot for ogling the mountains that tower above. The trail continues up and over Hannegan Pass—but that's the subject of a hiking guide.

18. Twin Lakes Road

RATING	⊛⊛⊛⊛⊛
DISTANCE	6.6 miles
ROAD SURFACE	Graded gravel/Not maintained
ROAD CONDITION	Good/Poor
ROAD GRADE	Extremely steep
PUCKER FACTOR	Valium prescribed
ACCESSIBLE	Summer, fall
LAND MANAGER/CONTACT	Mount Baker–Snoqualmie National Forest, Glacier Public Service Center, (360) 599-2714, www.fs.usda.gov/mbs
TRAILHEADS	Yellow Aster Butte, Tomyhoi Lakes, Winchester Mountain, High Pass, Skagway Pass
CAMPGROUNDS	Silver Fir
NOTES	Northwest Forest Pass ($5 daily, $30 annually) required

The Drive

This is the premier wild mountain drive in Washington, as far as I'm concerned. It's one road where the thrill of getting there nearly equals that of being there.

Getting There

Follow Highway 542 for 13.1 miles east from the Glacier Public Service Center to the Department of Transportation Equipment shed on the left. Turn left onto the Twin Lakes Road, Forest Road 3065, just east of the shed. (See map on page 48.) GPS location: N48°54.496'; W121°41.835'

The Road

The ease with which this drive begins belies the difficulties of the last 2.5 miles. I drove this road in a four-wheel-drive SUV and worried most of the way that it might not have the ground clearance to get across some of the rocky gullies or over big humps in the middle of switchbacks. I was so uncomfortable with the steep, open hillside that I couldn't look at the incredible view of Mounts Baker and Shuksan, just across the Nooksack River valley.

Yet when I reached mile-high Twin Lakes—which by no coincidence are two very similar alpine lakes—on a broad bench below 6,510-foot Winchester

Upper Twin Lake and the Winchester Mountain Trailhead from the parking area.

Mountain, I found several two-wheel-drive vehicles parked there, including a couple of compact cars. So if you're comfortable on steep mountain roads and good at negotiating rock-filled gullies, you'll like this road.

In any event, the drive up the first 4.4 miles to the Tomyhoi Lakes trailhead is on a wide, maintained gravel road and leads to essentially the same views of the surrounding mountains as you'll get from on high, so at least drive that far and check out the road ahead—you can see almost the entire route from the trailhead. In 2011, snow still covered portions of the road and Twin Lakes parking area in mid-September.

Begin by climbing, steeply at first, in view-hiding forest for about **1.0** mile to a switchback where the road levels a bit and winds above the Swamp Creek basin, reaching an old trail that climbs toward Yellow Aster Butte in **2.2** miles. The road turns and climbs along a sidehill to a second switchback and shortly after, switches back again to the Tomyhoi Lakes trailhead, **4.4** miles from the Mount Baker Highway. This trailhead is a popular one, with restrooms and parking for dozens of cars along the road.

Just beyond, you'll arrive at the open slopes and a sign indicating the road is not maintained beyond that point. Hikers sometimes park their autos here and walk the remaining 2.2 miles to Twin Lakes. I'd suggest you park here and take a look at what's ahead.

The road narrows from this point and begins to climb very steeply along the mountainside for 1.0 mile, crossing a gully carved by the creek that drains

Twin Lakes, about 1,000 vertical feet above, at **5.2** miles. In another 0.2 mile, you'll come to the first of six switchbacks, climbing about 800 feet in less than a mile. You'll round the final switchback on a broad saddle and drive around the southern Twin Lake to the parking area between the lakes. You're **6.6** miles from the Mount Baker Highway, but in an entirely different world.

Just above the lakes to the northwest is Winchester Mountain, where there's an old fire lookout you can reach by a steep 1.6-mile trail from the parking area. Mountains stretch in all directions and you can look north to the Cascades along the Canadian border and south to Mount Baker. The lakes hold trout and camping is permitted.

19. Skyline Divide Road

RATING	⊛⊛⊛
DISTANCE	12.7 miles
ROAD SURFACE	Paved/Graded gravel
ROAD CONDITION	Fair
ROAD GRADE	Moderate
PUCKER FACTOR	Flatlanders welcome
ACCESSIBLE	Summer, fall
LAND MANAGER/CONTACT	Mount Baker–Snoqualmie National Forest, Glacier Public Service Center, (360) 599-2714, www.fs.usda.gov/mbs
TRAILHEADS	Boyd Creek, Skyline Divide
NOTES	Northwest Forest Pass ($5 daily, $30 annually) required

The Drive

Here's a road that climbs from a river valley to an alpine trailhead with mountain views across the valley you've just ascended.

Getting There

Follow the Mount Baker Highway 542 a mile east of the Glacier Public Service Center and turn right on the Glacier Creek Road, Forest Road 39. GPS location: N48°53.393'; W121°55.396'

The Road

The Skyline Divide Road, Forest Road 37, joins the Glacier Creek Road, Forest Road 39, fewer than 100 feet from the Mount Baker Highway. Turn left, where you'll see a sign indicating that the Boyd Creek Trail is 3.0 miles away and the Skyline Divide Trail, 12.0 miles.

The road climbs around a low hill in forest before arriving alongside the Nooksack River at Horseshoe Bend, about **2.0** miles from the Mount Baker Highway. You'll drive about 1.0 mile farther before the pavement ends, **3.0** miles from the highway. Continue along the river for another 2.0 miles, passing inviting spots for picnicking and river-watching before switching back above Nooksack Falls, **5.0** miles from the highway. The road leaves the river here and begins to gain elevation in switchbacks, mostly in view-hiding forest where you would be wise to watch for deer on the road, especially early in the morning or just after sunset.

A creek tumbles from the mountains on the way to Skyline Divide.

The lowland forest begins to thin and change character as you climb, and shortly after crossing Deadhorse Creek, **8.0** miles from the highway, you'll find yourself amidst the hemlocks, with the views toward the ridge leading to 6,315-foot Church Mountain beginning to show more often through the trees.

You'll switchback all of 10 times, often on severely washboarded road, before crossing Cascade Creek at **11.5** miles, then climb around two more switchbacks before the road arrives at a wide trailhead parking area, 4,350 feet above sea level. Here you'll find a restroom and map kiosk. The cliffs of the Church Mountain ridge dominate the view to the north, and the view down the road to the west includes the Nooksack River valley and the mountains of the Mount Baker Wilderness.

The 3.5-mile Skyline Divide Trail leaves the parking area and climbs steeply to the south, gaining almost 2,000 vertical feet. It also gains great views of Mount Baker, hidden by foothills at the trailhead.

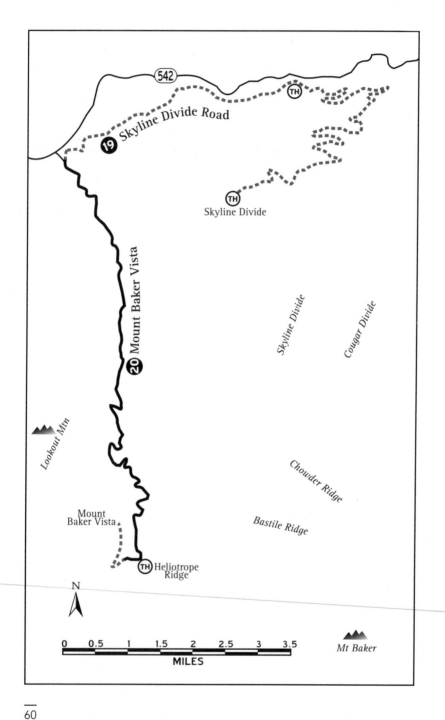

542

Skyline Divide Road

19

TH

Skyline Divide

Mount Baker Vista

20

Skyline Divide

Cougar Divide

Lookout Mtn

Chowder Ridge

Mount
Baker Vista

Bastile Ridge

TH Heliotrope
Ridge

N

0   0.5   1   1.5   2   2.5   3   3.5
MILES

Mt Baker

20. Mount Baker Vista

RATING	❀❀❀❀
DISTANCE	9.0 miles
ROAD SURFACE	Paved/Graded gravel
ROAD CONDITION	Fair
ROAD GRADE	Steep
PUCKER FACTOR	Sightseeing OK
ACCESSIBLE	Summer, fall
LAND MANAGER/CONTACT	Mount Baker–Snoqualmie National Forest, Glacier Public Service Center, (360) 599-2714, www.fs.usda.gov/mbs
TRAILHEADS	Heliotrope Ridge
NOTES	Northwest Forest Pass ($5 daily, $30 annually) required

The Drive

The view of the Coleman Glacier on 10,781-foot Mount Baker doesn't get any better than this unless you're willing to climb a steep 3-mile trail leading to the toe of the glacier.

Getting There

Follow the Mount Baker Highway 542 a mile east of the Glacier Public Service Center and turn right on the Glacier Creek Road, Forest Road 39. (See map on page 60.) GPS location: N48°53.393'; W121°55.396'

The Road

I would have given this drive a 5-star rating were it not for the bumpy gravel portions of the road and the fact that in most years, you can follow the Mount Baker Highway 542 to Artist Point, where the view of the mountain is equal to the one you'll get from the Mount Baker Vista. On some maps the place is called Glacier Viewpoint, but whatever you call it, it's an awe-inspiring view.

Begin by immediately passing the junction with the Skyline Divide Road, Forest Road 37 (drive #19), on the left and following the Glacier Creek canyon upstream. You'll climb above the stream for 2.9 miles before crossing it and following the west side of the canyon for about 1.5 miles. The road enters a young forest as the canyon narrows, turns, and begins to climb out of the valley, 4.3 miles from the highway. You may be able to see cliffs called the Palisades across the canyon.

Mount Baker from the Baker Vista Road, just below the viewpoint.

The road alternates between gravel and pavement, with the paved areas mostly on switchback corners and across bridges. The transition between pavement and gravel is where you'll find the biggest potholes. You'll arrive at the first of several creek crossings at Coal Creek, **4.5** miles; followed by Falls Creek, **4.9** miles; and Lookout Creek, **5.3** and **5.7** miles from the Mount Baker Highway.

Beyond, drive to a junction with Forest Road 36 on the right, **7.9** miles from the highway. Stay left and round a corner above Grouse Creek to the Heliotrope Ridge trailhead, **8.0** miles. The Heliotrope Ridge Trail is both a hiking and climbing trail that leads to a Coleman Glacier overlook as well as giving mountaineers access to the glacier on their way to the summit of Mount Baker. It's a steep path that crosses a number of streams that must be forded.

Past the trailhead, the road continues to climb and switches back before arriving at the Vista, where you'll find a picnic area and restroom. And, as mentioned in the beginning, a splendid view of Mount Baker.

NORTH CASCADES HIGHWAY 20

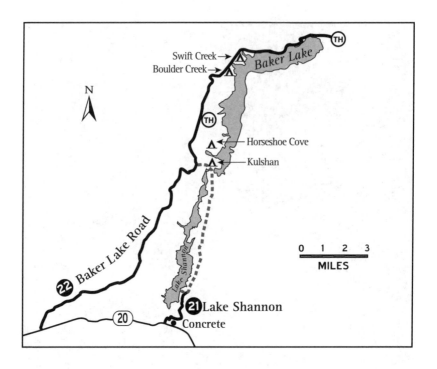

21. Lake Shannon

RATING	◉◉
DISTANCE	3.5 miles to boat launch; 12.0 miles to Baker Lake Road
ROAD SURFACE	Paved/Graded gravel
ROAD CONDITION	Good/Poor
ROAD GRADE	Steep
PUCKER FACTOR	Flatlanders welcome
ACCESSIBLE	Spring–fall
LAND MANAGER/CONTACT	Puget Sound Energy, Baker River Recreation, (360) 853-8341, pse.com /aboutpse/ToursandRecreation
NOTES	Quiet, unpopulated picnic or boat-launching spot. Good paddling location.

The Drive

Here's a short drive leading to a boat launch and picnic area, with an option of driving a rough, muddy road around Shannon Lake to the Baker Lake Road, 12 miles north.

Getting There

From downtown Concrete, off Highway 20 (watch the speed trap!), turn left on the Baker Road and cross the Baker River. GPS location: N48°32.378'; W121°44.684'

The Road

Beyond the Baker River Bridge, the road switches back and climbs out of the river canyon to a second hairpin corner where there's an excellent view of the Lower Baker River Dam, operated by Puget Sound Energy. The dam is 285 feet high and holds 7.0-mile-long Lake Shannon, a nice lake for paddling that is basically unpopulated along the eastern shore. It's popular with anglers, who find trout and sockeye salmon from the hatchery below the Upper Baker River Dam.

Past the hairpin, the paved road ends and climbs around a forested hill and arrives at a junction with the private Everett Lake Road, **1.4** miles from Concrete. Keep left at the junction and drive along the west shore of the small lake, where you may see a variety of waterfowl along the shoreline. The road narrows in a forest of mixed fir and alder, generally following power lines

The Lower Baker Dam creates Lake Shannon.

from the upper dam. The openings in the forest made by the lines yield the only views of the lake below.

At **2.9** miles, you'll arrive at a junction with a road leading downhill to the left, signed "Public Boat Launch." Turn left here and drive 0.6 mile downhill to the lake and boat launch with a restroom. A short road leads north along the shoreline, where you'd likely find a good spot for a picnic.

Back at the junction, you can turn left and follow the road another 12.0 miles to the junction with the Baker Lake Road (drive #22) at Koma Kulshan Guard Station, crossing the Upper Baker River Dam at **10.5** miles. The road has numerous unsigned junctions and traverses logged and some muddy areas even in midsummer. If you choose to try this road, I'd suggest you turn around and drive it from the other end, which is less confusing and the way I drove it.

22. Baker Lake Road

RATING	⊕⊕⊕
DISTANCE	26.1 miles
ROAD SURFACE	Paved/Graded gravel
ROAD CONDITION	Good
ROAD GRADE	Moderate
PUCKER FACTOR	Flatlanders welcome
ACCESSIBLE	Spring–fall
LAND MANAGER/CONTACT	Puget Sound Energy, Baker River Recreation, (360) 853-8341, pse.com/aboutpse /ToursandRecreation; Mount Baker– Snoqualmie National Forest, Mount Baker Ranger District, (360) 856-5700 ext. 515, www.fs.fed.us/mbs
TRAILHEADS	Shadow of the Sentinels, Baker River, Baker Lake
CAMPGROUNDS	Kulshan, Horseshoe Cove, Boulder Creek, Swift Creek
NOTES	Northwest Forest Pass ($5 daily, $30 annually) required

The Drive

The Baker Lake Road, Forest Road 11, passes one of the nicest lakes and outdoor recreation areas in northwestern Washington, with lakefront campgrounds and picnic areas, paddling and boating, mountain views and hiking trails.

Getting There

From Sedro-Woolley, drive 15 miles east to the Baker Lake Road at Birdsview and turn left. (See map on page 64.) GPS location: N48°31.944'; W121°50.207'

The Road

Baker River tumbles off its namesake Mount Baker and rattles into 9.0-mile-long Baker Lake, and this road traverses its western shoreline. While anglers, paddlers, and campers follow this road to enjoy the lake, climbers and hikers join them for hikes and mountaineering on the south-facing slopes of the 10,781-foot snow giant to the north. Die-hard skiers and snowboarders find the open slopes great riding almost until the new winter snows begin to fall.

Cross the Upper Baker Dam to drive around Lake Shannon.

The drive begins by following the Grandy Creek valley up a hillside past Grandy Lake, about **4.3** miles from the North Cascades Highway 20. The mile-long lake has a private campground and is a favorite spot for RVers in big rigs. At **6.8** miles, pass the junction with a road leading to Lake Tyee on the right and continue to the Bear Creek Bridge at **9.9** miles. Arrive at the Mount Baker–Snoqualmie National Forest boundary in another long 1.0 mile and pass a junction with Forest Road 12 at **12.9** miles.

So far, you haven't glimpsed a sign of Baker Lake, but that all changes at **13.9** miles, where a junction with a road passing Koma Kulshan Guard Station winds through evergreen forest to the Puget Sound Energy's Kulshan Campground at the Upper Baker River Dam. The facility is open year-round for camping, one of more than a half dozen campgrounds along the road. These offer ample opportunities for day-use and picnicking along the lake.

Back on the Baker Lake Road, continue north, passing the easy Shadow of the Sentinels interpretive trail at **14.4** miles. (Hint: Big trees abound.) The right turn to Horseshoe Cove Campground is next, **15.1** miles from the North Cascades Highway. If you're not ready to stop yet, drive another 2.7 miles to Boulder Creek Campground. Stay right at a junction with Forest Road 1130, and pass a road leading to Panorama Point, which—as you've probably guessed by now—has spectacular views, **19.3** miles from the North Cascades Highway.

Just past the junction is a road leading down to the Swift Creek Campground, mile **20.3**. This was once the old Baker Lake Resort, now managed as a Forest Service campground. The pavement ends just beyond and the road begins to angle toward the shoreline, climbing only to cross Chadwick Creek and passing a road to a campground and boat launch at **23.6** miles. The road continues along the shoreline, where several wide pullouts offer pleasant picnic spots or "diverse" camping.

About 0.5 mile from the end of the road, you'll leave the lake and drive into the forest at the north end of the lake to the Baker Lake and Baker River trailheads, where the road ends **26.1** miles from the North Cascades Highway. If you have binoculars, check out the high cliffs of Mount Hagan, above the trees to the east. Also, the wide, barrier-free level trail begins with a pleasant 0.5-mile stroll to a nicely designed bridge across the Baker River, with views up the river and ridges leading west to the big mountain itself.

23. Hart's Pass Road

RATING	⚙⚙⚙⚙⚙
DISTANCE	19.2 miles
ROAD SURFACE	Paved/Graded gravel
ROAD CONDITION	Good
ROAD GRADE	Extremely steep
PUCKER FACTOR	Valium prescribed
ACCESSIBLE	Summer, fall
LAND MANAGER/CONTACT	Okanogan-Wenatchee National Forest, Methow Valley Ranger District, (509) 996-4003, www.fs.fed.us/r6/okanogan
TRAILHEADS	Pacific Crest, Haystack Mountain
CAMPGROUNDS	Gate Creek, Ballard, Rivers Bend, Hart's Pass, Meadow
NOTES	Northwest Forest Pass ($5 daily, $30 annually) required. Trailers prohibited on Hart's Pass Road. Wildflower programs in summer.

The Drive

Ride to a beautiful, wide alpine bench where you can see the North Cascade Mountains, visit one of the highest auto campgrounds in the state, walk on a trail that stretches from Mexico to Canada, and—for a real thrill—drive on the highest public road in Washington.

Getting There

From Highway 20, turn right to Mazama and turn left on the Lost River Road. GPS location: N48°35.543'; W120°24.301'

The Road

Gold and silver ore lured miners to build the road to Hart's Pass more than 115 years ago, where at least 1,000 residents lived in a community just west of the 6,198-foot-high pass. Today, the treasure of the splendid view, annual wildflower programs, and the opportunity to drive the steep, airy Slate Peak Lookout Road—the highest road where you can drive a car in Washington—draws visitors from throughout the state and beyond.

The drive begins with a paved stretch along the scenic Methow River, passing riverfront homes and an airstrip underneath the Goat Wall, a massive cliff ridge that appears to lean over the valley from the northeast. The wall is

The Slate Peak Lookout Road climbs from Hart's Pass below.

home to both the animals for which it is named and hundreds of rock climbers who gather for what they term "fun in the sun."

At **6.8** miles, you'll cross the Lost River Bridge and run out of pavement just beyond, then pass the Ballard Campground on the right, **8.8** miles from the highway. At **9.2** miles, you'll reach a junction with the Hart's Pass Road, Forest Road 5400, which switches back to the right and begins its steep climb to the pass. Elevation at this point is 2,628 feet, so you'll be gaining more than 3,500 feet in the next 10.0 miles.

That climb becomes immediately apparent as the road is carved from a cliff wall with views into the Methow River valley below. In 3.0 miles, you'll round Deadhorse Point, 1,000 feet above the river valley. From here, you can look across the valley to the peaks of the North Cascades, down the valley to the Goat Wall, and north up the road to a notch in the mountains near Hart's

Pass. Mountain goats can often be seen on cliffs above the road—and sometimes even on the byway.

At mile **15.1**, you'll pass an avalanche chute at Tozier Creek and beyond find a bit of relief from the climb as you pass alpine meadows below the road at Layout Camp, **16.3** miles from Mazama. Mule deer frequent the meadows, and visitors with binoculars might spot bear in the high country.

The road continues to climb through alpine meadows, reaching Hart's Pass at **19.2** miles. The Hart's Pass Guard Station is staffed during the summer and there's a small campground at the pass. The nicer Meadow Campground can be found about 1.0 mile to the left on Forest Road 5400-500, which climbs past the campground and ends at a Pacific Crest Trail trailhead—the last road access to the trail until it reaches Canada.

If you haven't had enough of steep roadside cliffs or amazing views, turn right at Hart's Pass on the Slate Peak Lookout Road, Forest Road 5400-600, which is the highest public road in Washington. It climbs open mountainside for 2.6 miles to a gate just below 7,440-foot-high Slate Peak, where there's a Forest Service lookout listed on the National Register of Historic Places. The trail to the lookout is steep, but less than 0.25 mile. The lookout is no longer staffed on a full-time basis and you'll find a spectacular 360-degree view of North Cascade peaks that include Mount Baker and Jack Mountain to the west and Silver Star to the south. Look north into British Columbia and northeast into the vast Pasayten Wilderness.

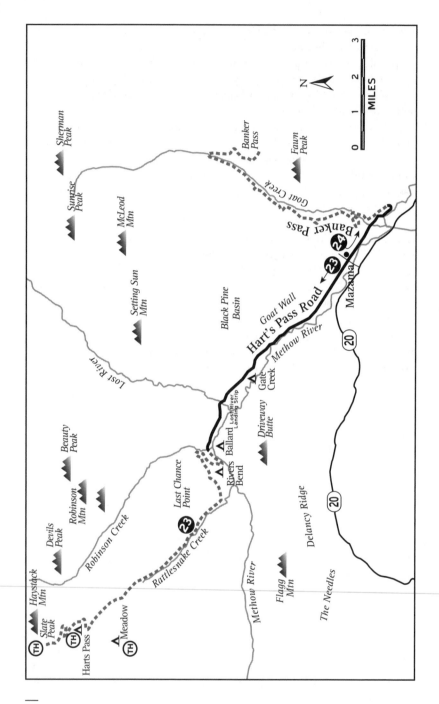

24. Banker Pass

RATING ●●
DISTANCE 12.6 miles
ROAD SURFACE Graded gravel
ROAD CONDITION Fair
ROAD GRADE Steep
PUCKER FACTOR Sightseeing OK
ACCESSIBLE Spring–fall
LAND MANAGER/CONTACT Okanogan-Wenatchee National Forest,
Methow Valley Ranger District,
(509) 996-4003, www.fs.fed.us/r6/okanogan
NOTES Dusty in summer

The Drive

This popular snowmobiling route in the winter is a good drive in the summer to an open mountain slope overlooking the valley and North Cascade peaks.

Getting There

From Highway 20, turn right to Mazama and then turn right on Goat Creek Road. (See map on page 74.) GPS location: N48°35.543'; W120°24.301'

The Road

The paved road passes riverfront homes on the right in the community of Mazama and hillside farms and homes on the left. Drive **1.4** miles southeast to a junction with Forest Road 52, and turn left onto the gravel road.

The Goat Creek Sno-Park is on your right at **2.0** miles and the road is closed here in the winter for snowmobiling. The route is regularly groomed all the way to Banker Pass and beyond. The road usually holds snow at its upper reaches until spring, and it's a good idea to check the conditions before taking this drive.

The route climbs gently from the Sno-Park, winding in open pine forest above Goat Creek, on your left. At mile **3.0**, you'll drop down and cross the creek, then switchback twice up steep hillside where you can look down the creek valley. The road now climbs along the hillside past a junction with Forest Road 500 on the left, **4.6** miles from Mazama. You'll get views up the Goat Creek valley as the road alternately passes through forest and open slopes and at **7.0** miles, you'll turn into a steep gully and cross Whiteface Creek. Drive another 3.4 miles to Vanderpool Crossing, where the road swings around a wide switchback, crosses the creek, and begins climbing toward Banker Pass.

The Goat Creek Sno-Park is popular with snowmobile riders heading to Banker Pass.

The road enters open hillside below the pass, with views to the valley below and across to 6,577-foot Fawn Peak. This is a good spot to turn around, although motorists seeking a longer drive can continue on FR 52 as it drops down to the Cub Creek Road, eventually joining the Chewuch River Road to Winthrop.

25. Chewuch River Road

RATING	●●●●
DISTANCE	27.6 miles
ROAD SURFACE	Paved/Graded gravel
ROAD CONDITION	Excellent/Good
ROAD GRADE	Moderate
PUCKER FACTOR	Flatlanders welcome
ACCESSIBLE	Summer, fall
LAND MANAGER/CONTACT	Okanogan National Forest, Methow Valley Ranger District, (509) 996-4003, www.fs.fed.us/r6/okanogan
TRAILHEADS	Andrews Creek, Thirtymile
CAMPGROUNDS	Falls Creek, Chewuch, Camp Four, Andrews Creek
NOTES	Northwest Forest Pass ($5 daily, $30 annually) required

The Drive

This road leads through beautiful pine forest to the scene of one of the largest wildfires in recent history, and to the memorial for the firefighters who lost their lives fighting it.

Getting There

From the main intersection in the town of Winthrop on Highway 20, follow the Chewuch Road north out of town. A sign points north to Pearrygin Lake State Park. GPS location: N48°28.658'; W120°11.106'

The Road

This drive on Forest Roads 51 and 5160 follows the Chewuch River upstream past a number of campgrounds to trails leading into the vast Pasayten Wilderness and the Thirtymile Memorial. This roadside stop honors four young forest firefighters, killed a decade ago when the Thirtymile Fire struck them down with superheated air as they huddled in their emergency shelters. It's a powerful place to visit, decorated with the hats, shirts, and other mementos left by fellow firefighters from throughout the country.

The blaze began as a picnic cooking fire on July 9, 2001, and the picnickers who started it have never been identified. It spread to 25 acres overnight and exploded to more than 9,300 acres before it was brought under control.

Blackened forest covers the mountainside above the memorial for the fallen firefighters.

Killed were Tom Craven, Karen Fitzpatrick, Jessica Johnson, and Devin Weaver. Several campers were trapped when the fire burned across the road, and six people suffered burn injuries.

Head out of town on the Chewuch Road, passing the Pearrygin Lake Road **1.6** miles from Winthrop. Stay left, and at **6.7** miles, turn left and cross a bridge over the Chewuch. Turn right at the junction past the bridge, and at **7.5** miles, you'll enter Okanogan National Forest on Forest Road 51, which is paved.

Keep right at the junction with Forest Road 5130 and drive through a forest of giant pines along the river. Stay right, again, at a junction with Forest Road 5140, **10.8** miles from Winthrop.

The first campground, Falls Creek, features a number of riverfront campsites, **12.1** miles from Winthrop. You'll find the Chewuch Campground next, then Camp Four Campground, **18.2** miles from Winthrop.

Stay left on Forest Road 5160 at a junction **19.0** miles from Winthrop (you can return to Winthrop on the other side of the river on Forest Road 5010 on the way back). Just past the junction, you'll be able to see the charred evidence of the Thirtymile Fire on the mountains above.

Pass the Crystal Lake and Lake Creek Trail signs, and at **24.0** miles, find the Andrews Creek trailhead. The road, now Forest Road 250, turns to gravel just across the Andrews Creek bridge, and there's a nice campsite by the river.

Beyond, the gravel road climbs a bit and enters the area blackened by the Thirtymile blaze. The memorial is on the left, **27.6** miles from Winthrop.

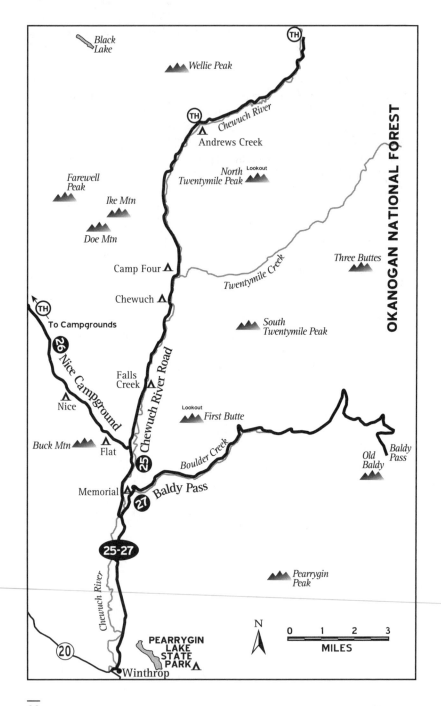

26. Nice Campground

RATING	⊕⊕⊕
DISTANCE	13.4 miles
ROAD SURFACE	Paved/Graded gravel
ROAD CONDITION	Good
ROAD GRADE	Moderate
PUCKER FACTOR	Flatlanders welcome
ACCESSIBLE	Summer, fall
LAND MANAGER/CONTACT	Okanogan National Forest, Methow Valley Ranger District, (509) 996-4003, www.fs.fed.us/r6/okanogan
TRAILHEADS	Copper Glance Lake
CAMPGROUNDS	Flat, Nice, Ruffed Grouse, Honeymoon
NOTES	Northwest Forest Pass ($5 daily, $30 annually) required

The Drive

Huge ponderosa pines greet you at this quiet campground along Pine Creek, a fine picnic and fishing spot.

Getting There

From the main intersection in the town of Winthrop on Highway 20, follow the Chewuch Road north out of town. A sign points north to Pearrygin Lake State Park. (See map on page 80.) GPS location: N48°28.658'; W120°11.106'

The Road

I'll admit it: I chose this drive because I liked the name "Nice Campground." Turns out it was named accurately. Drive out of town on the Chewuch Road, passing the Pearrygin Lake Road **1.6** miles from Winthrop. Stay left, and at **6.7** miles, turn left and cross a bridge over the Chewuch. Turn right at the junction past the bridge, and at **7.5** miles, you'll enter Okanogan National Forest on Forest Road 51, which is paved.

At **9.5** miles, you'll reach the junction with Forest Road 5130 and turn left. In another 0.5 mile, you'll pass a junction with Forest Road 5130-100, which climbs to Buck Lake in about 2.0 miles. Stay right and continue another 1.0 mile, crossing Eightmile Creek. You'll pass Flat Campground, the first of four campgrounds along FR 5130, **11.6** miles from Winthrop.

Continue on FR 5130 past a junction with 5130-300 at **11.8** miles, where the road turns to gravel above Deer Creek. Giant pines shade the road, which, in

Ponderosa pine trees tower above accurately named Nice Campground.

another 1.6 miles, arrives at Nice Campground on the left. Pretty campsites above the creek invite a picnic, while a pool upstream where Deer and Eight-mile Creeks join looks like a good fishing hole.

For a longer drive, you can continue to Ruffed Grouse Campground, **17.4** miles from Winthrop, or Honeymoon Campground at **18.5** miles. The road passes the Copper Glance Lake trailhead at **22.2** miles, and ends at a corral and unimproved mining road at **25.5** miles.

27. Baldy Pass

RATING	❂❂❂❂
DISTANCE	25.0 miles
ROAD SURFACE	Paved/Graded gravel
ROAD CONDITION	Good
ROAD GRADE	Steep
PUCKER FACTOR	Sightseeing OK
ACCESSIBLE	Summer, fall
LAND MANAGER/CONTACT	Okanogan National Forest, Methow Valley Ranger District, (509) 996-4003, www.fs.fed.us/r6/okanogan
NOTES	Good views east at pass

The Drive

Here's a scenic climb up steep-walled canyons to a 6,400-foot-high pass where you'll see evidence of a huge forest wildfire.

Getting There

From the main intersection in the town of Winthrop on Highway 20, follow the Chewuch Road north out of town. A sign points north to Pearrygin Lake State Park. (See map on page 80.) GPS location: N48°28.658'; W120°11.106'

The Road

You'll find more dramatic views than the one from Baldy Pass, but few places serve up such consistently nice weather at such high altitudes. The pass would make an excellent spot for a sunset picnic and a star-watching adventure, where no city lights shine to ruin the stellar show. Just make certain you've got good headlights for the drive back down the mountain.

Drive north from Winthrop on the Chewuch Road, passing the Pearrygin Lake Road **1.6** miles from Winthrop. Stay left, and at **6.7** miles arrive at a junction with the Forest Road 37 to Baldy Pass. Turn right and begin climbing up the rocky Boulder Creek canyon for 4.0 miles to a junction with Forest Road 800 at the Bromas Creek crossing, **14.0** miles from Winthrop. Turn right here and cross the creek.

The road continues to climb and the views begin to get wider as you enter the Bernhardt Creek valley and, at **19.5** miles, reach a junction with Forest Road 39. Turn right here, and continue on FR 37 as it climbs steeply above the middle fork of Boulder Creek, finally crossing the creek at **22.5** miles.

The road from Baldy Pass traverses steep mountainside burned in a 2006 wildfire.

Here FR 37 begins to climb more steeply again in alpine forest, reaching Baldy Pass **25.0** miles from Winthrop.

The summit of Old Baldy Mountain, 7,844 feet high, is just 0.8 mile to the south. From the pass, you can look to the southeast where a 2006 forest fire, one of the largest fires in Okanogan National Forest history, burned to within miles of the lakeside community of Conconully. You can return the way you came, or continue on Forest Road 37 for about 18.0 miles to Conconully.

HIGHWAY 97

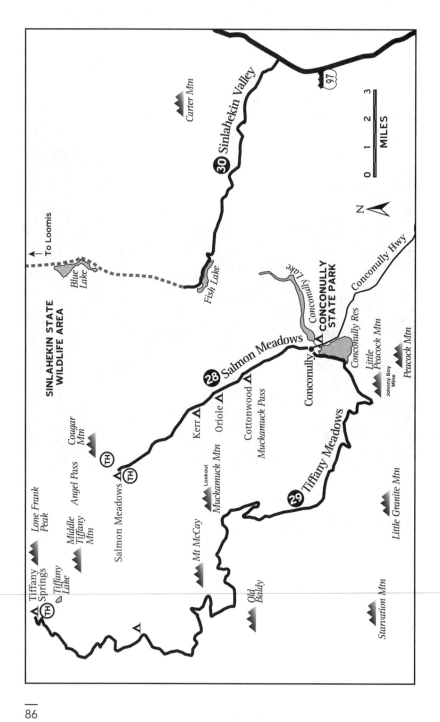

28. Salmon Meadows

RATING	⊛⊛⊛⊛
DISTANCE	8.5 miles
ROAD SURFACE	Paved
ROAD CONDITION	Good
ROAD GRADE	Moderate
PUCKER FACTOR	Flatlanders welcome
ACCESSIBLE	Summer, fall
LAND MANAGER/CONTACT	Okanogan-Wenatchee National Forest, Tonasket Ranger District, (509) 486-2186, www.fs.fed.us/r6/okanogan
TRAILHEADS	Clark Ridge, Freezeout, Angel Pass
CAMPGROUNDS	Cottonwood, Oriole, Kerr, Salmon Meadows
NOTES	Northwest Forest Pass ($5 daily, $30 annually) required

The Drive

Take this short ride from the community of Conconully to a high country meadow, a wildflower haven and former site of a Civilian Conservation Corps ski lodge.

Getting There

Drive to Conconully and head west on Forest Road 38 from the intersection with the road leading to Lake Conconully Resort. GPS location: N48°33.630'; W119°45.014'

The Road

Few places that are accessible by road are as pretty as the griddle-flat Salmon Meadows. Though located below timberline, the grassy green field 4,400 feet above sea level has the feel of the alpine meadows found in mountains 3,000 feet above. It's a wonderful picnic spot in the summer.

The road climbs out of the lake basin in timberland, with the middle fork of Salmon Creek chattering beside the road on the left. At **1.8** miles, the road enters the Okanogan National Forest and a little more than 0.25 mile farther, passes the Cottonwood Campground on the left. The road now climbs more steeply above the creek to a junction with a road that drops down to the Oriole Campground, **2.6** miles from Conconully.

Keep left at a junction with Forest Road 3810, **3.4** miles from the town, as the road continues to climb in a forest changing from pine to fir as it gains

Salmon Meadows on a summer day.

elevation. You'll pass Kerr Campground at **4.3** miles and just beyond, the road dips at the site of a washout in 2011, then begins climbing again. At **7.2** miles, stay left at a junction with a forest road leading up Milk Creek, climb the steepest hill yet, and arrive at Salmon Meadows at **8.5** miles.

You'll find a road junction as you enter the meadows, so climb the road to the right into the broad grassland. A road leads west to a wide trail to the site of the old Salmon Meadows Ski Lodge, built by the Civilian Conservation Corps during the Great Depression. The lodge burned to the ground more than 20 years ago and several Conconully residents tried unsuccessfully to rebuild it.

Trails also lead from Salmon Meadows to Angel Pass, about 2.0 miles, and to Tiffany Lake, about 6.0 miles.

29. Tiffany Meadows

RATING	🎬🎬🎬
DISTANCE	30.7 miles
ROAD SURFACE	Paved/Graded gravel
ROAD CONDITION	Good
ROAD GRADE	Steep
PUCKER FACTOR	Sightseeing OK
ACCESSIBLE	Summer, fall
LAND MANAGER/CONTACT	Okanogan-Wenatchee National Forest, Tonasket Ranger District, (509) 486-2186, www.fs.fed.us/r6/okanogan
TRAILHEADS	Bernhardt, Freezeout Ridge, South Twentymile, Tiffany Lake
CAMPGROUNDS	Tiffany Springs
NOTES	Northwest Forest Pass ($5 daily, $30 annually) required

The Drive

The road to Tiffany Meadows climbs up and around some of the prettiest mountains in the Okanogan to green meadows stretching to a beautiful alpine lake, just a short walk from a primitive campground.

Getting There

From the entrance to Conconully State Park, follow the lakeshore road around the west side of the Conconully Reservoir past Shady Pines Resort and the Okanogan National Forest boundary. (See map on page 86.) GPS location: N48°33.425'; W119°45.971'

The Road

The last time I took this drive was in the fall of 2010, on my way to a backpacking trip to Black Lake, in the Pasayten Wilderness. My friend Dan Weaver—aka The Big Scribe—and I figured it would be a shortcut to the Pasayten via Baldy Pass (drive #27). It turned out to be a much longer trip than we anticipated, but also one of the best Sunday drives I've enjoyed in a long time. I tried to revisit the road in June 2011, but Baldy Pass was still closed by snow.

Pass lakefront cabins on the left and just beyond the Shady Pines Resort—where, as you might expect, huge pines provide plenty of shade—round a corner to start up the west and south forks of Salmon Creek, **1.3** miles from

Tiffany Lake is a short walk from Tiffany Meadows.

Conconully. The road enters Okanogan National Forest and at **3.0** miles, turns right up Forest Road 37 and climbs along a pine-covered ridge. It crosses Rusty Creek at **5.5** miles and at **8.4** miles, arrives at a junction with roads leading up the west fork of Salmon Creek and McCay Creek, where you'll stay left on FR 37. Keep right at the next junction, **9.9** miles from Conconully, continuing on FR 37. The road switches back at **11.5** miles and again 1.0 mile later, where you'll get views of 7,844-foot-high Old Baldy and its blackened forest, ravaged by a huge forest fire in 2006.

The road climbs under cliffs and gullies where you can look up to Pelican Pass, about **14.0** miles from Conconully, and 7,454-foot Mount McCay on the right, where a big rockslide once partially blocked the road and has now been cleared, **16.0** miles from Conconully. You'll reach Baldy Pass at **17.8** miles, where the view toward the Okanogan Valley is more than impressive. From here, the road winds down the Bernhardt Creek valley to a junction with Forest Road 39. Turn right on FR 39 and begin climbing again as mountaintops peek at you from the tops of a fir and tamarack forest.

The road rounds a broad switchback at **24.9** miles, where swampy Rogers Lake, just above the road, affords a good view of Tiffany Mountain, the highest point in Okanogan at 8,242 feet. Beyond, the road climbs around a forested pass at **26.7** miles, where you'll find the Freezeout Ridge trailhead. This

1.8-mile path leads to the open slopes of Tiffany Mountain, and is the shortest route of several Tiffany trails to the summit.

The road drops to Brown Meadows, which are anything but that color in the summer, before climbing to Tiffany Meadows, **29.4** miles from Conconully and 6,100 feet above sea level. The South Twentymile Trail begins here, and the meadows make a good spot for a picnic, especially after the first freeze slows down the mosquito and blackfly armies of the summer.

Motorists wishing to drive beyond can climb two switchbacks and another long 1.0 mile to the Tiffany Springs Campground, **30.7** miles from Conconully. This primitive campground has sites with picnic tables and fire rings, as well as a restroom. Those who feel up to a short 1.0-mile walk downhill to beautiful Tiffany Lake will find the trailhead just across the road from the campground.

Forest Road 39 continues past the campground, eventually climbing up and over Lone Frank Pass and dropping to connect with Forest Road 38 at Salmon Meadows (drive #28). The road is rough and Forest Service officials suggest only vehicles with high clearance and four-wheel drive attempt this route back to Conconully.

30. Sinlahekin Valley

RATING	⊛⊛⊛⊛
DISTANCE	14.0–36.0 miles
ROAD SURFACE	Paved/Graded gravel
ROAD CONDITION	Good
ROAD GRADE	Moderate
PUCKER FACTOR	Sightseeing OK
ACCESSIBLE	Summer, fall
LAND MANAGER/CONTACT	Washington Department of Fish and Wildlife, Omak District Office, (509) 826-4626, www.wdfw.wa.gov
CAMPGROUNDS	Fish Lake, Blue Lake
NOTES	Discover Pass ($10 daily; $30–$35 annually) required if parking

The Drive

The road through the sunny Sinlahekin Valley leads past clear high lakes filled with trophy rainbow trout, where white-tailed deer gallop in wide meadows.

Getting There

Follow Highway 97 north from Omak for 5.9 miles to the Pine Creek Road and turn left onto Pine Creek Road. (See map on page 86.) GPS location: N48°34.509'; W119°32.040'

The Road

If you've only a short day for this drive, plan to visit Fish and Blue Lakes, returning via the Conconully Road to Okanogan and Highway 97. If you've all day, take the entire drive from Highway 97 and through the Sinlahekin Valley to the village of Loomis, then past Spectacle and Whitestone Lakes to Tonasket and return to Highway 97.

The road begins in wide-open sageland, punctuated with big pine trees and massive rock hillsides, climbing past ranches and farms where well-kept lawns stretch like emerald flags against the golden fields. At **5.5** miles, reach a junction with the North Pine Creek Road and stay left on the pavement. The road is now the Fish Lake Road.

After driving another 2.1 miles, you cross into the Sinlahekin Wildlife Area, a haven for a variety of birds and animals. You'll swing around a corner and pass Mud Lake below and on your left, then reach a viewpoint high above Fish Lake, **8.3** miles from your starting point. Fish Lake is stocked by

Blue Lake, an angler's paradise, lies at the center of the Sinlahekin Valley.

the Department of Fish and Wildlife annually, and makes an excellent choice for anglers who camp at a number of Department wildlife access sites along the lake. Most anglers fish from small boats or float tubes, but several spots along the shore often yield equally good results for trout lovers.

The road turns to gravel at **9.2** miles, then winds down around a sharp corner and junction with the Stalder Road, where you'll stay left and in another 1.0 mile, reach a junction with a bumpy, washboarded road leading to Conconully. Stay right and begin your tour up the Sinlahekin Valley, where pine forests rise on either side of the road. At **11.8** miles, you'll pass a pull-through campsite and outhouse used mainly by hunters and equestrians where back-country trails lead into the hills.

The byway climbs slightly in the next 1.0 mile and views open to the hills in the east and west, tattooed with black basalt slides. Crest a hill at **13.8** miles and look down on beautiful Blue Lake, the destination for anglers who catch (and release) rainbow trout almost large enough to tow them around in their float tubes. The first access and launch for small boats is **13.9** miles from Highway 97, and campsites there make for sunny picnicking and a good spot to turn around.

The area around Blue Lake is also an excellent spot for wildlife-watching. You'll see raptors circling above as well as deer and perhaps black bear in the meadows and hillsides above the lake. Watch your step: this is rattlesnake country.

If you turn around, consider following the Okanogan National Forest road to Conconully at its junction with the Fish Lake Road. The road is rough and moderately steep in some areas, but leads through nice forestland and along the scenic unpopulated end of the Upper Conconully reservoir. Follow the Conconully Road back to Highway 97 in Omak or Okanogan.

Drivers wishing to continue from Blue Lake can follow the road north above the lake and cross Sinlahekin Creek (which sometimes washes the road out in spring). The route heads north past Forde and Conners Lakes before leaving the wildlife area. You'll pass farmland before reaching Loomis, where you'll turn right and drive past Spectacle and Whitestone Lakes before turning south to Tonasket and Highway 97.

HIGHWAY 2

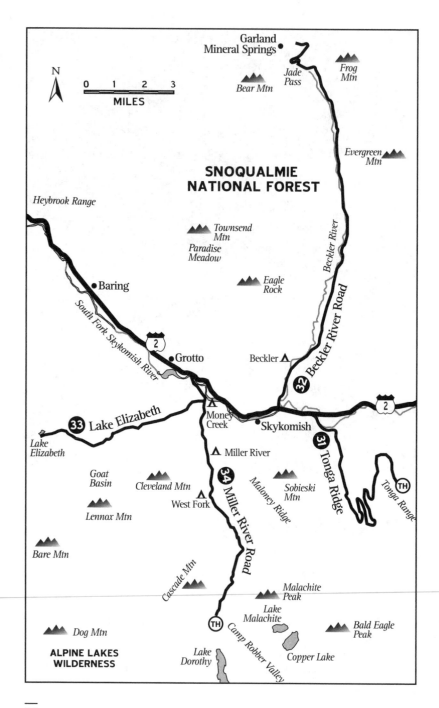

31. Tonga Ridge

RATING	❷❷
DISTANCE	11.2 miles
ROAD SURFACE	Paved/Graded gravel
ROAD CONDITION	Good
ROAD GRADE	Moderate
PUCKER FACTOR	Flatlanders welcome
ACCESSIBLE	Spring–fall
LAND MANAGER/CONTACT	Mount Baker–Snoqualmie National Forest, Skykomish Ranger District, (360) 677-2414, www.fs.fed.us/mbs
TRAILHEADS	Tonga Ridge
CAMPGROUNDS	Foss River
NOTES	Northwest Forest Pass ($5 daily, $30 annually) required

The Drive

Climb from river valley through forest to a high ridge overlooking the Sky-komish Valley. Visit in the fall for the berry harvest.

Getting There

From Skykomish, drive 1.9 miles east on Highway 2 and turn right onto the Foss River Road. GPS location: N47°42.730'; W121°19.269'

The Road

Tonga Ridge might be better named Huckleberry Heaven, because it's one of the closest places for many of us to find those plump little sweet treats that grow on bushes. Best time to take this drive is around late summer and early fall—but you'd better get there early or someone else will pick all the berries closest to the trailhead.

The road follows the Foss River for about **1.0** mile before turning left and crossing the watercourse on a one-lane bridge and entering the Mount Baker–Snoqualmie National Forest and gaining the designation Forest Road 68. The pavement ends **1.1** mile from Highway 2, and you'll follow the river upstream to the junction with Forest Road 6830, **3.2** miles from the highway. Turn left here, and begin climbing in a series of switchbacks to the Tonga Ridge trailhead.

You'll be traveling through deep evergreen forest and patches of recently logged timber, where views open to the Foss River valley below and south to

Cascade Mountains look down on the Tonga Ridge Trailhead.

the Alpine Lakes Wilderness. The road climbs to the first of seven switchbacks at **4.3** miles, then climbs in forest for another 1.0 mile before switching back again. A third switchback, above Burnt Creek at **6.6** miles, looks across a recently logged section to the peaks in the wilderness.

The road continues to climb, rounding another wide switchback and passing through a recently logged forest where you can look across the Foss River valley above Skykomish, then rounds a corner to a junction with Forest Road 6830-310, **9.9** miles from the highway. Turn right on this spur road and follow it for 1.3 miles to the Tonga Ridge trailhead, 4,341 feet above sea level. The best berry-picking can be found about 0.5 mile up a steep trail at the boundary of the Alpine Lakes Wilderness.

32. Beckler River Road

RATING	●●
DISTANCE	15.2 miles
ROAD SURFACE	Paved/Graded gravel
ROAD CONDITION	Good
ROAD GRADE	Moderate
PUCKER FACTOR	Flatlanders welcome
ACCESSIBLE	Spring–fall
LAND MANAGER/CONTACT	Mount Baker–Snoqualmie National Forest, Skykomish Ranger District, (360) 677-2414, www.fs.fed.us/mbs
TRAILHEADS	Blanca Lake, Quartz Creek
CAMPGROUNDS	Beckler River
NOTES	Northwest Forest Pass ($5 daily, $30 annually) required

The Drive

Here's a very pleasant trip up a pretty river, passing a forest campground with river valley views.

Getting There

Follow Highway 2 for 0.75 mile east of the bridge leading to the community of Skykomish to the Beckler River Road and turn north. (See map on page 96.) GPS location: N47°42.877'; W121°20.671'

The Road

In the fall, the Beckler River is low and clear as it rolls into the Skykomish River just east of Skykomish. The road follows the river upstream into a steep, forested canyon before it climbs to 2,589-foot Jack Pass.

Begin by following the road north for **1.0** mile to a bridge crossing the river and turning up the east bank. Enter the Mount Baker–Snoqualmie National Forest, where the road becomes Forest Road 65. At mile **1.5**, pass the Beckler River Campground on the left, where there's quiet riverside camping amidst huge firs and cedars, far enough from Highway 2 that traffic noise won't keep you awake.

The paved road climbs along, just above the river in alder and fir forest, with views up and down the river to 4,000-foot peaks on either side. The pavement ends at a river crossing **7.2** miles from Highway 2, where the road

The Beckler River flows past the Beckler River Campground.

joins Forest Road 6520. Turn left across the bridge, then right on FR 65, where a sign indicates that the Index-Galena Road is closed, 10.0 miles ahead.

Beyond, FR 65 enters the narrow, steep Beckler River canyon and crosses the river at **8.3** miles, climbing to a crossing with Bullbucker Creek, **9.1** miles from the highway. Pass a junction on the left at **12.0** miles and climb the steepest part of the road to Jack Pass, **13.0** miles from the highway. Stay on FR 65 as it drops in steep switchbacks to the North Fork of the Skykomish River, joining Forest Road 63 at mile **15.2**, your turnaround point. This road is closed by flood damage downstream and provides access to two trailheads upstream.

33. Lake Elizabeth

RATING	⊕⊕⊕
DISTANCE	7.7 miles
ROAD SURFACE	Paved/Graded gravel
ROAD CONDITION	Fair
ROAD GRADE	Moderate
PUCKER FACTOR	Sightseeing OK
ACCESSIBLE	Spring–fall
LAND MANAGER/CONTACT	Mount Baker–Snoqualmie National Forest, Skykomish Ranger District, (360) 677-2414, www.fs.fed.us/mbs
TRAILHEADS	Lake Elizabeth Loop
CAMPGROUNDS	Money Creek
NOTES	No Northwest Forest Pass required at lake

The Drive

This is an excellent spot for families and seniors who can't or won't walk a long trail to a lake, and is the only lake in the Skykomish Ranger District that is accessible by car.

Getting There

Drive Highway 2 to the Old Cascade Highway bridge crossing to the Money Creek Campground and turn south across the bridge, 2.9 miles west of the Skykomish village bridge. (See map on page 96.) GPS location: N47°43.838'; W121°24.554'

The Road

The road to Lake Elizabeth is a popular one with local residents, but doesn't draw big crowds of hikers simply because the trail to the lake is nothing more than a short walk. Families with young children and grandparents are sure to enjoy picnics on sunny days at the lake.

Begin by passing the Money Creek Campground, with campsites on either side of the road and riverside sites to the right, and drive **1.0** mile east to the Miller River Road. Turn right and drive a short block to the Money Creek Road, Forest Road 6420, and turn right again. You'll cross Money Creek in about 0.5 mile, where the pavement ends and the road begins climbing in alder forest above the creek. The thick forest prevents all but peekaboo views down to the creek or to the hills above.

The road to Lake Elizabeth crosses Money Creek.

You'll continue to climb through forest and logged-over areas, where the braided channels of Money Creek open the forest and yield better views. The road begins to climb more steeply after about **4.0** miles, then switches back twice and traverses on forested hillside far above the creek. At **6.8** miles, the road gets rougher as it rounds a corner where the hillside below is open, then arrives at Lake Elizabeth, **7.7** miles from Highway 2.

A short trail leads around the lake. Because there are no developed amenities at the lake, no Northwest Forest Pass is required.

34. Miller River Road

RATING	⊛⊛⊛
DISTANCE	10.2 miles
ROAD SURFACE	Paved/Graded gravel
ROAD CONDITION	Good
ROAD GRADE	Moderate
PUCKER FACTOR	Flatlanders welcome
ACCESSIBLE	Summer, fall
LAND MANAGER/CONTACT	Mount Baker–Snoqualmie National Forest, Skykomish Ranger District, (360) 677-2414, www.fs.fed.us/mbs
TRAILHEADS	Lake Dorothy
CAMPGROUNDS	Money Creek, Miller River, West Fork
NOTES	Northwest Forest Pass ($5 daily, $30 annually) required

The Drive

Drive up a shining river, through a leafy forest, and into a tumbling creek before reaching the edge of the Alpine Lakes Wilderness and a steep, short trail leading to Lake Dorothy.

Getting There

Drive Highway 2 to the Old Cascade Highway bridge crossing to the Money Creek Campground and turn south across the bridge, 2.9 miles west of the Skykomish village bridge. (See map on page 96.) GPS location: N47°43.838'; W121°24.554'

The Road

The Miller River Road is probably the best ride to the mountains and lakes at the edge of the Alpine Lakes Wilderness. Look down the river valley to the Cascade Mountains surrounding the valley or take a short but steep walk to Lake Dorothy, the closest of the Alpine Lakes in the Stevens Pass corridor.

Begin by passing the Money Creek Campground, with campsites on either side of the road and riverside sites to the right, and drive **1.0** mile east to the Miller River Road, Forest Road 6410. Turn right and continue past the junction with the Money Creek Road (drive #33), where the pavement ends. You'll be driving through a lowland forest above the river for 3.1 miles, where you'll pass a road leading down to the river and the Miller River Group Campground. Beyond, you'll cross a bridge and at **4.7** miles, cross the West Fork

The Miller River Road climbs out of the forest to the Lake Dorothy Trailhead.

of the Miller River, where the road designation changes to Forest Road 6412. Stay left on FR 6412.

The road now begins to climb, winding along above the valley for about 3.0 miles before turning and crossing the West Fork, **7.1** miles from the highway. The road climbs and switches back again, passing a recently logged area on the left, and dives into the forest. In about 1.0 mile, you'll drive into a creek and cross the water on a concrete ramp. Beyond, the road climbs again and the forest opens to reveal the valley below and Cascade peaks above. At **10.2** miles, you'll arrive at the trailhead, which was enlarged and received a brand-new outhouse in August 2011.

The trail to Lake Dorothy is a steep one, climbing 1.0 mile into the Alpine Lakes Wilderness. Those seeking a picnic spot and a shorter walk might climb to the bridge at Camp Robber Creek, about 0.5 mile from the trailhead.

35. Iron Goat Wayside

RATING	❀❀
DISTANCE	6.6 miles
ROAD SURFACE	Paved
ROAD CONDITION	Good
ROAD GRADE	Moderate
PUCKER FACTOR	Flatlanders welcome
ACCESSIBLE	Spring–fall
LAND MANAGER/CONTACT	Mount Baker–Snoqualmie National Forest, Skykomish Ranger District, (360) 677-2414, www.fs.fed.us/mbs; www.irongoat.org
TRAILHEADS	Iron Goat
NOTES	Northwest Forest Pass not required at Wayside; required at Wellington and Martin Creek trailheads

The Drive

The best part of this short drive is the beginning, at the Iron Goat Interpretive Wayside, a beautifully restored Great Northern caboose.

Getting There

Drive to milepost 58.3 on Highway 2 and turn north, where you'll see a bright red caboose and a large parking area on the right. GPS location: N47°42.686'; W121°09.793'

The Road

It isn't so much the drive that makes this an inviting place to slow down on your way up or back from Stevens Pass, but the chance to see a piece of history and take a relaxing drive along the Tye River back to Highway 2. After leaving the highway, turn right into the parking area and take a gander at the old caboose there. You can read about the history of the Great Northern Railway and the engineering that went into crossing the Cascade Mountains at Stevens Pass, more than 100 years ago.

You can also visit trailheads at the beginning and end of the 6.0-mile-long Iron Goat Trail from Martin Creek to Wellington (drive #36). Both of these trailheads feature barrier-free pathways along the old roadbed.

Once you've read all about it, drive across the entrance road to the Old Cascade Highway, which follows the Tye River downstream above its northern bank. You'll be in deep evergreen forest, with views of the river cascades and

A Great Northern caboose now decorates the Iron Goat Wayside.

peeks at cars speeding along Highway 2 on the opposite side of the river. The road winds downhill **1.5** miles to a junction with Forest Road 6710. To see the beginning of the Iron Goat Trail at Martin Creek, turn right here and follow the gravel road for 1.4 miles to the trailhead.

It's a good spot for a picnic and a chance to stretch your legs along the Iron Goat Trail. The wide, graded path follows the old railroad route through snowsheds and is a gentle climb, barrier free for almost 3.0 miles. Back on the Old Cascade Highway, turn downhill and wind through forest for another 2.3 miles to its junction with Highway 2.

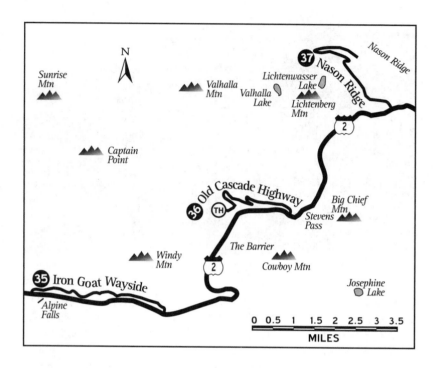

36. Old Cascade Highway: Stevens Pass to Wellington

RATING	⚙⚙⚙
DISTANCE	2.9 miles
ROAD SURFACE	Paved
ROAD CONDITION	Fair
ROAD GRADE	Steep
PUCKER FACTOR	Sightseeing OK
ACCESSIBLE	Summer, fall
LAND MANAGER/CONTACT	Mount Baker–Snoqualmie National Forest, Skykomish Ranger District, (360) 677-2414, www.fs.fed.us/mbs
TRAILHEADS	Iron Goat
NOTES	Northwest Forest Pass ($5 daily, $30 annually) required

The Drive

This short road leads to the site of one of the most tragic railroad disasters in the nation's history.

Getting There

Follow Highway 2 to Stevens Pass, where the Old Cascade Highway joins Highway 2 from the north, about 150 yards west of the summit. Visibility at the junction is extremely limited, given highway speeds, so motorists coming from the west should continue to the summit, then turn around and drive back to the junction. (See map on page 110.) GPS location: N47°44.757'; W121°05.631'

The Road

The year 1910 was not a good one for Northwesterners. On March 1, a wall of snow 10 feet high, 0.25 mile wide, and 0.5 mile long raged down the open slopes of Windy Mountain and smashed two trains trapped at the Wellington Depot 150 feet down the mountainside. Ninety-six people were killed, making it the deadliest avalanche in American history. Later that year, the largest wildfire in U.S. history scorched parts of Washington, Idaho, and Montana, killing 87 people and turning a forest about the size of Connecticut into charcoal.

An accessible trail follows the old railroad grade from the historic community of Wellington, the scene of the 1910 avalanche.

By following the Old Cascade Highway down from Stevens Pass at milepost 64.4, you can drive to the site of the Wellington Depot, where the avalanche hit. You'll find interpretive signs and restrooms and the beginning of the Iron Goat Trail, which follows the roadbed of the old Great Northern Railway down the Tye River valley for 6.0 miles. It's a short walk of about 0.3 mile down the trail to the first of several snowsheds the railroad built following the tragedy. Though the path is crushed rock, it is accessible to those in wheelchairs, with assistance.

The Old Cascade Highway switches back through shady forest and at **2.9** miles, you turn right at a junction with the short access road to Wellington. Motorists can continue down the Old Cascade Highway to a bridge across the Tye River, which is closed to all but bicycle traffic.

37. Nason Ridge

RATING	⚙⚙⚙
DISTANCE	4.0 miles
ROAD SURFACE	Graded gravel
ROAD CONDITION	Good
ROAD GRADE	Steep
PUCKER FACTOR	Sightseeing OK
ACCESSIBLE	Summer, fall
LAND MANAGER/CONTACT	Okanogan-Wenatchee National Forest, Wenatchee River Ranger District, (509) 548-2550, www.fs.usda.gov/okawen
TRAILHEADS	Smith Brook
NOTES	Late snow keeps road closed until summer

The Drive

This is the scenic, alpine way to get from Stevens Pass to Lake Wenatchee without driving Highway 2, or simply to take a 4-mile drive to a viewpoint atop Nason Ridge.

Getting There

Follow Highway 2 to mile 68.7, the Smith Brook Road, and turn north. East and westbound lanes at this intersection are separate, and eastbound motorists can turn left on the Smith Brook access road, crossing the westbound lanes to the Smith Brook Road. (See map on page 110.) GPS location: N47°47.006'; W121°02.399'

The Road

The drive to a saddle on Nason Ridge, that forested alpine spine of the Cascades that stretches from Stevens Pass to Lake Wenatchee, is a pleasant climb up a valley to a timberline view of the Cascade Mountains in all directions. You can extend the drive by continuing another 23.0 miles north and east to Lake Wenatchee (drive #38).

The Smith Brook Road, Forest Road 6700, starts high and climbs higher into the Cascade Mountains—higher, in fact, than Stevens Pass by nearly 600 feet. It's a beautiful drive to the 4,623-foot-high pass at Nason Ridge and one that makes an excellent outing after the crowds of summer have left and before the snow falls.

The road crosses a bridge and climbs from its beginning at 3,200 feet above sea level along the Smith Brook (also called Smithbrook) valley where

Snowbanks hang out along the road to Nason Ridge as late as mid-July.

mountains swoop down from the west and across the valley to the east. You'll round a couple of switchbacks before crossing to the west side of the valley and climbing past the Smith Brook trailhead, **2.8** miles from the highway. The Smith Brook Trail is a 1.0-mile-long climb to a junction with the Pacific Crest Trail, which stretches from Canada to Mexico.

Beyond the trailhead parking area, the road makes a sweeping switchback in open alpine slopes where you can look down the valley and up the road for 1.0 mile to the Nason Ridge. This section of the road often holds snow until late spring, and climbs steeply to the notch in Nason Ridge, where there's a wide place to park and turn around, above a tiny ridgetop snowmelt pond.

38. Rainy Creek Road

RATING	⊛⊛⊛⊛
DISTANCE	9.3 miles
ROAD SURFACE	Graded gravel
ROAD CONDITION	Good
ROAD GRADE	Steep
PUCKER FACTOR	Sightseeing OK
ACCESSIBLE	Summer, fall
LAND MANAGER/CONTACT	Okanogan-Wenatchee National Forest, Wenatchee River Ranger District, (509) 548-2550, www.fs.usda.gov/okawen
TRAILHEADS	Snowy Creek, Lake Minotaur
CAMPGROUNDS	Riverside
NOTES	Late snow keeps road closed until summer

The Drive

From a 4,600-foot-high pass on Nason Ridge, follow Forest Road 6700 down the scenic Rainy Creek valley to the Little Wenatchee River Road and Lake Wenatchee.

Getting There

From Highway 2 at mile 68.7, follow the Smith Brook Road, Forest Road 6700, north for 4 miles to a pass at Nason Ridge (drive #37). GPS location: N47°48.056'; W121°03.460'

From Lake Wenatchee, follow the Little Wenatchee River Road, Forest Road 65, west for 6.3 miles to its junction with Forest Road 6700. GPS location: N47°50.994'; W120°56.593'

The Road

This is a scenic and relaxed route from Stevens Pass to Lake Wenatchee, one where traffic isn't likely to be a problem and you can drive as slowly as you like without drawing angry looks or worse, vulgar gestures. Deer are likely to be as plentiful along this road as other vehicles, so keep a lookout.

Begin at the top of Nason Ridge (drive #37) and drop steeply to the north and east on Forest Road 6700 for **1.0** mile to a junction with Forest Road 6705 at a sharp hairpin and keep left. Forest Road 6705, to the right, leads to the Snowy Creek trailhead, a steep climb along Nason Ridge.

From a high viewpoint on the Rainy Creek Road, look down on where you've been.

Just around the hairpin to the left, you'll find an excellent viewpoint looking down the Rainy Creek valley. See that road, way down there? You'll be there in a few minutes.

The road continues to wind downward and the grade eases along the straight stretch you saw from above, **2.6** miles from Nason Ridge. Beyond, you'll pass a road leading to the Lake Minotaur trailhead, **2.9** miles from the ridge. The road now drops again to a meadow and crosses a creek and waterfall **6.2** miles from Nason Ridge. It then winds down to the Little Wenatchee River, passing a junction with Forest Road 6701 on the left, **8.9** miles from the ridge and just beyond it, the Riverside Campground, before crossing the Little Wenatchee River and joining Forest Road 65. Turn right for Lake Wenatchee.

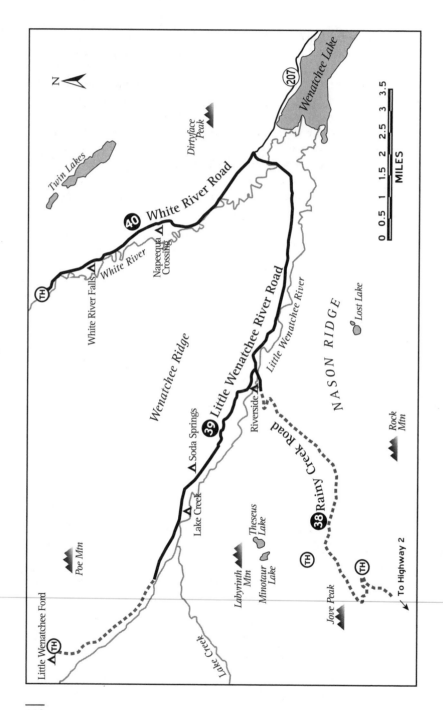

39. Little Wenatchee River Road

RATING	●●
DISTANCE	15.4 miles
ROAD SURFACE	Paved/Graded gravel
ROAD CONDITION	Good
ROAD GRADE	Moderate
PUCKER FACTOR	Flatlanders welcome
ACCESSIBLE	Spring–fall
LAND MANAGER/CONTACT	Okanogan-Wenatchee National Forest, Wenatchee River Ranger District, (509) 548-2550, www.fs.usda.gov/okawen
TRAILHEADS	Cady Creek, Poe Mountain Lookout
CAMPGROUNDS	Soda Springs, Lake Creek, Little Wenatchee Ford
NOTES	Northwest Forest Pass ($5 daily, $30 annually) required

The Drive

Here's a scenic route above a green river valley into the forest and end-of-the-road camping.

Getting There

From Highway 2 at the Lake Wenatchee junction, follow the Lake Wenatchee Highway 207 north and west around the lake to its junction with the White River Road and Little Wenatchee River Road and turn left onto the Little Wenatchee River Road. (See map on page 118.) GPS location: N47°51.069'; W120°49.882'

The Road

You'll cross the White River in about **0.25** mile, with a view of the White Mountains upstream, and in **1.4** miles, the county road ends and Little Wenatchee River Road becomes Forest Road 65. At **4.1** miles, stay left at a road that climbs to a viewpoint and continue for another 2.2 miles to a junction with Forest Road 6700 (drive #38). Keep right here, where the paved road narrows to one lane with turnouts, climbing into forest above the river **7.6** miles from Lake Wenatchee.

The road passes a junction with the Soda Springs Campground at **7.8** miles and you'll keep right as it climbs to a second junction at **8.9** miles. Keep left here, crossing Devil's Club Creek—named for a thoroughly nasty bush—and

The Little Wenatchee River Road crosses the White River at River Bridge Campground.

arriving at the Lake Creek Campground at **10.5** miles. The road continues to climb above the river, now a narrow stream, to a junction with a road climbing to the right at **12.8** miles.

The pavement ends here, and the road beyond is steep and rocky. Stay left and continue to the end of the road at the Little Wenatchee Ford Campground. Trails heading up Cady Creek and the Poe Mountain Lookout begin at this campground.

40. White River Road

RATING	●●
DISTANCE	10.5 miles
ROAD SURFACE	Paved/Graded gravel
ROAD CONDITION	Good
ROAD GRADE	Moderate
PUCKER FACTOR	Flatlanders welcome
ACCESSIBLE	Spring–fall
LAND MANAGER/CONTACT	Okanogan-Wenatchee National Forest, Wenatchee River Ranger District, (509) 548-2550, www.fs.usda.gov/okawen
TRAILHEADS	White River
CAMPGROUNDS	Napeequa Crossing, White River Falls
NOTES	Northwest Forest Pass ($5 daily, $30 annually) required

The Drive

Enjoy a drive up a river valley settled more than 100 years ago, where you'll find huckleberry hunting, wildlife, and a side trip to an impressive viewpoint.

Getting There

From Highway 2 at the Lake Wenatchee junction, follow the Lake Wenatchee Highway 207 north and west around the lake to its junction with the White River Road and Little Wenatchee River Road, and bear right on the White River Road. (See map on page 118.) GPS location: N47°51.069'; W120°49.882'

The Road

Settlers came to the White River valley more than 100 years ago and Native Americans lived here long before that. Game was plentiful—and still is—and huckleberries covered the hillsides. The White River Road, Forest Road 6400, is marked with signs for a self-guided auto tour, with the first stop **1.2** miles from the Little Wenatchee River Road at the gravesite of one of the first settlers in the valley, Eunice Henry.

Stay left at a junction with a road leading to Tall Timber Ranch at **2.6** miles, and at **2.9** miles, find Forest Road 6403, which climbs steeply about 900 vertical feet in 2.3 miles to an overlook on Dirtyface Peak. Back on the White River Road, you'll arrive at Napeequa Crossing Campground, **6.3** miles, and run out of pavement in another 0.1 mile.

The White River Road ends at the White River Trailhead.

Beyond, at mile **8.1**, you'll pass the area where Wenatchee Indians crossed the river to hunt game and pick huckleberries. The area is still popular with huckleberry hounds. The road passes Grasshopper Meadows at **8.4** miles, where I was unable to find either a grasshopper or a meadow, although there was a nice aspen grove.

White River Falls Campground is at mile **9.5**, where you can get a view of the 132-foot-high cascade. Drive another 1.0 mile to road's end, the White River trailhead, and a footbridge across Indian Creek. Drivers looking to stretch their legs can follow trails up both sides of the river under a canopy of ancient cedars and firs.

41. Chiwawa River Road

RATING	✪✪✪✪
DISTANCE	25.2 miles
ROAD SURFACE	Paved/Graded gravel
ROAD CONDITION	Good
ROAD GRADE	Moderate
PUCKER FACTOR	Flatlanders welcome
ACCESSIBLE	Summer, fall
LAND MANAGER/CONTACT	Okanogan-Wenatchee National Forest, Wenatchee River Ranger District, (509) 548-2550, www.fs.usda.gov/okawen
TRAILHEADS	Chickamin Ridge, Basalt Ridge, Schaefer Lake, Rock Creek, Little Giant, Trinity
CAMPGROUNDS	Grouse Creek, Riverbend, Rock Creek, Schaefer Creek, Atkinson Flats, Nineteen Mile, Alpine Meadows, Phelps Creek
NOTES	Northwest Forest Pass ($5 daily, $30 annually) required

The Drive

Head into the heart of the hills on the sunny side of the Cascade Mountains up a wide river valley dotted with green alpine meadows.

Getting There

Follow the Lake Wenatchee Highway 207 north from Highway 2 to the Chiwawa Loop Road and turn right. GPS location: N47°49.692'; W120°41.988'

The Road

They might have named this road the Avenue of the Campgrounds, because you'll find enough campsites to house everyone in Seattle who owns a tent. Well, almost. The nice part is, you can forget your rainfly and not get wet. Well, most of the time. Truly, this is the sunny side of the state and the camping here is a whole lot different from plastic tarp–festooned campsites you'll find on the wet west side of the Cascades.

The road heads east and in **0.5** mile, passes the other half of the Chiwawa Loop Road on the left. Stay right and at **1.3** miles, reach the Chiwawa River Road, Forest Road 62. Turn left and note the mileage sign to Trinity, the site of a private mining operation. After driving another 3.0 miles, you'll enter

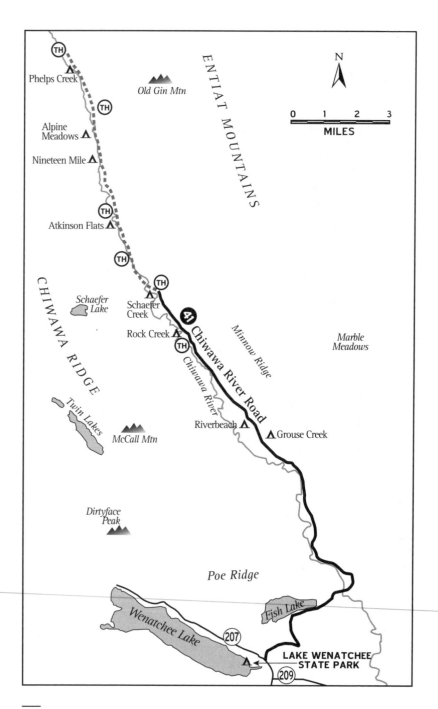

the Chiwawa River Recreation Area, with its many trails, campgrounds, and off-road vehicle routes.

Goose Creek is the first campground you'll pass at **5.1** miles, but certainly not the best unless you've come to enjoy the many motorcycle trails that radiate from the camping area. Next comes Grouse Creek, at **10.3** miles on the left. The road narrows to one lane with turnouts at **11.8** miles, at a junction with trails leading to Chickamin Ridge on the right. Stay left and continue for another 0.5 mile to the end of the pavement.

You'll arrive at the Rock Creek Guard Station at **15.3** miles, where there's a water supply, restroom, and an information kiosk with a map of the Chiwawa Recreation Area. A trail here climbs steeply east to Basalt Ridge. Just down and across the road is the Schaefer Lake trailhead. Next you'll pass the Riverbend Campground at **16.6** miles. Here is the site of one of the prettiest camping spots in the valley, with a river and mountain view that is difficult to beat.

The Rock Creek trailhead is 0.1 mile farther up the road, followed by the Rock Creek Campground, **17.0** miles from the Lake Wenatchee Highway. Pass the Chiwawa Horse Camp and Schaefer Creek Campground in another 0.5 mile, where the rocky road of the last several miles improves noticeably. Atkinson Flats is next in the campground army, at **19.5** miles, then comes Nineteen Mile Campground, which according to my odometer, is at **21.3** miles. No matter.

After driving by the Little Giant trailhead, you'll pass Alpine Meadows Campground, another favorite of mine, at **23.2** miles. Finally, at **25.0** miles, pass the Phelps Creek Campground in high, open meadows and fragrant alpine forest. In another 0.2 mile, you'll arrive at the Trinity trailhead and parking area. The road is gated and posted with a "Private Property" sign just beyond.

The valley around Trinity is splendid, with views to the high mountains on either side of the Chiwawa, now a rushing, tumbling stream. It's a great place to get away from the heat in the valleys below, slap at mosquitoes, and watch deer browse in the meadows in the morning.

Early morning on the Chiwawa River Road.

42. Icicle Creek Road

RATING ❂❂❂❂
DISTANCE 14.5 miles
ROAD SURFACE Paved/Graded gravel
ROAD CONDITION Good
ROAD GRADE Moderate
PUCKER FACTOR Flatlanders welcome
ACCESSIBLE Spring–fall
LAND MANAGER/CONTACT Okanogan-Wenatchee National Forest,
Leavenworth Ranger Station,
(509) 548-6977, www.fs.usda.gov/okawen
TRAILHEADS Snow Creek, Fourth of July, Icicle Gorge
CAMPGROUNDS Eightmile, Johnny Creek, Ida Creek, Chatter
Creek, Rock Island, Black Pine
NOTES Northwest Forest Pass ($5 daily, $30
annually) required

The Drive

This is a sunny Sunday outing for anyone visiting Leavenworth who would like to get into the mountains without fighting the traffic along Stevens Pass.

Getting There

From Highway 2 in Leavenworth, turn south on the Icicle Creek Road. GPS location: N47°35.286'; W120°40.479'

The Road

Because it starts in the popular tourist town of Leavenworth, the Icicle Creek Road likely sees more traffic than some of the other wild roads in the Okanogan-Wenatchee National Forest. Still, you might park in the middle of the road to watch a deer or scan the cliffs above for rock climbers of both the two- and four-legged variety without fear of getting rear-ended by the nut who thinks he can see the sights while driving at 35 miles an hour. He'll probably be texting, as well.

Hikers, rock climbers, anglers, campers, and white-water kayakers all use the Icicle Creek Road to gain access to one of the most beautiful areas of the Central Cascade Mountains. Icicle Creek plunges down a steep, rocky canyon where the peaks hover above. The upper sections of this road follow the creek in a wide valley shaded by giant pine trees.

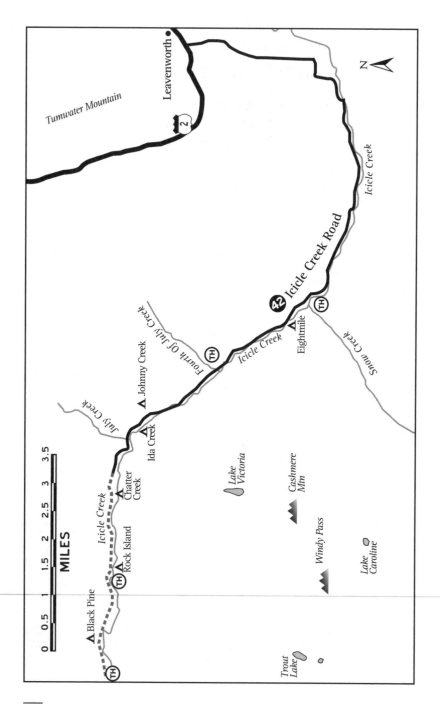

The Icicle River rages along the Icicle River Road.

Begin by driving south past private homes and crossing the Icicle River in **0.5** mile. The neighborhood continues south for more than 1.0 mile before it gains a rural feel and passes the Leavenworth National Fish Hatchery at **2.1** miles. For an interesting afternoon, turn left on Fish Hatchery Road to the visitor center here, which is open throughout the year and celebrates the return of salmon with a festival, usually the last weekend of September. For hours of operation, visit www.fws.gov/leavenworth.

Beyond, the road climbs above the canyon and leaves the crowds behind. You'll pass the end of the county road, **4.3** miles from the highway at the Snow Creek trailhead. This steep trail leads to the two Snow Lakes in the Alpine Lakes Wilderness and is popular with both hikers and rock climbers, who challenge the 700-foot-high Snow Creek Wall, a mighty rock formation on the south side of Snow Creek.

In another 4.0 miles, you'll pass a road leading to the Eightmile Campground. Riverside sites there are popular with white-water kayakers and rock climbers, as well as westside campers looking for some sunshine. In another 0.7 mile, you'll arrive at a junction with the Eightmile Road, Forest Road

7601, which crosses Icicle Creek and climbs on the world's most washboarded road to two trails leading to Eightmile Lakes and Stuart Lake.

Next, drive another 2.0 miles to the Fourth of July trailhead on the right, one of the steepest trails along Icicle Creek. Hikers looking for a 5.0-mile-long workout select this trail in the early season because it tends to melt out earlier than trails on the north side of the canyon. The road continues another 2.0 miles to the Johnny Creek Campground, a good spot for a picnic **12.2** miles from Leavenworth. Drive past the campground to the end of the pavement at **13.5** miles and continue another 0.5 mile, where you'll find Ida Creek Campground at the confluence of Icicle and Ida Creeks. This is a pleasant, quiet campground that is wheelchair accessible.

A new section of road was under construction at **14.5** miles, a good spot to turn around, in the summer of 2011. If work is complete, you can drive to Chatter Creek Campground, **16.5** miles from Leavenworth, and the Icicle Gorge trailhead, a gentle 4.0-mile loop trail between the campground and Rock Island Campground, **19.0** miles from Leavenworth. The road branches above Rock Island Campground. To the right, 1.5 miles beyond, the road ends at Black Pine Campground, while the left fork ends in 1.4 miles.

HIGHWAYS 970 AND 97

43. Teanaway River Road

RATING	❂❂❂❂❂
DISTANCE	23.6 miles
ROAD SURFACE	Paved/Graded gravel
ROAD CONDITION	Fair
ROAD GRADE	Moderate
PUCKER FACTOR	Sightseeing OK
ACCESSIBLE	Summer, fall
LAND MANAGER/CONTACT	Wenatchee National Forest, Cle Elum Ranger District, (509) 852-1100, www.fs.usda.gov/okawen
TRAILHEADS	Esmeralda Basin
CAMPGROUNDS	Twentynine Pines, Beverly
NOTES	Northwest Forest Pass ($5 daily, $30 annually) required

The Drive

This road on the sunny side of the state climbs into the heart of the Cascade Mountains to the home of Washington's newest wolf family, the Teanaway Pack. A short trail at road's end leads to one of the prettiest alpine wildflower shows in the state.

Getting There

Take the Cle Elum exit 85 from I-90 and follow Highway 970 east for 6.6 miles to the Teanaway Road and turn left. GPS location: N47°11.771'; W120°46.373'

The Road

Besides being one of the best roads leading to alpine vistas and wildflower walks, this is a rare opportunity for a chance to see wolves in the wild. The Teanaway wolf pack has at least four adult members, and Washington Department of Fish and Wildlife believes pups were born to the pack in 2011. This road is one of the few spots where you might catch a glimpse of one of these critters without leaving your vehicle. In fact, one of the well-known photos of a Teanaway wolf was taken near Liberty. That historic gold mining community (drive #47) is a couple miles off Highway 97, the Swauk Pass highway.

The lower portions of the Teanaway Road pass through green farmland and country estates, with the last opportunity for civilized shopping at the

The Esmeralda peaks rise above the Teanaway River Road.

Teanaway Mercantile, **6.7** miles from Highway 970. Here, a sign announces that "ice, candy, beer, and more" is available. Part of the "more" is a Northwest Forest Pass, which you'll need if you plan to picnic at any one of several campgrounds along the river.

Keep right at the junction with the West Fork Teanaway Road, **7.4** miles from the highway, and stay left at the junction with Forest Road 9738 at **13.0** miles. You'll reach the end of the pavement at **13.5** miles, at the Twentynine Pines Campground.

Keep right on Forest Road 9737 to Esmeralda Basin and enter the Okanogan-Wenatchee National Forest at **14.7** miles. Keep left at the Stafford Creek junction with Forest Road 9703, and in another 2.6 miles, stay right at a junction with the Trail 1391 Road. Follow FR 9737 left across a bridge to Beverly Campground, **17.7** miles from the highway. Beverly is one of the nicer campgrounds, with sites along the Teanaway.

A logging operation was under way in the summer of 2011, which was both good and bad. It was good because the rough, dusty road was recently graded and watered by the logging contractor. And it was bad because logging trucks are big and difficult to miss if you're driving too fast.

At **21.9** miles, you'll pass Camp Wahoo, a unique summer camp for youngsters who learn to care for the horses they "adopt" for the length of their stay. Keep right at the next road junction, following FR 9737 to its end at the Esmeralda Basin trailhead. The trailhead itself is scenic, surrounded by 7,000-foot peaks and its own cascading waterfall.

The Esmeralda Basin Trail climbs about 250 feet in the first 0.2 mile, passes a junction with the steep Longs Pass Trail at 0.4 mile, then enters the Esmeralda Basin, where you're certain to see wildflowers and perhaps even a wolf.

44. Swauk Pass West

RATING	✦
DISTANCE	4.0 miles
ROAD SURFACE	Graded gravel
ROAD CONDITION	Fair
ROAD GRADE	Moderate
PUCKER FACTOR	Sightseeing OK
ACCESSIBLE	Summer, fall
LAND MANAGER/CONTACT	Wenatchee National Forest, Cle Elum Ranger District, (509) 852-1100, www.fs.usda.gov/okawen
NOTES	Watch for wildlife. Brushy along road.

The Drive

This road accesses two excellent viewpoints looking northwest to the Alpine Lakes Wilderness.

Cascade peaks of the Alpine Lakes Wilderness shine from the forest road west of Swauk Pass.

Getting There

From Highway 97 at Swauk Pass, turn west into the parking area to the forest road leading uphill at the northwest end of the parking area. GPS location: N47°20.188'; W120°34.828'

The Road

The plan was to follow Forest Road 7324 downhill from Swauk Pass to Scotty Creek Campground, but this plan turned to mush 0.6 mile from the pass, where I found a sign telling me that FR 7324 was closed 2.5 miles beyond due to a washout. So much for planning. There was nothing to do but follow Forest Road 7324-800 to the left, into the brush.

I really had no idea where the road went and couldn't find it on my pathetic road atlas. (Hint: Get yourself an official Forest Service Motor Vehicle Use Map. Even though they are unwieldy, huge things that identify major forest roads in impossibly small type, they at least include every road in the forest.)

But things turned out all right, as they usually do. At **2.5** miles, you'll look across the valley below to one of several rock towers that make this a popular climbing area, and at **3.3** miles, find a wide parking area where you have an excellent view of the Cascade Mountains that guard the Alpine Lakes Wilderness. The road ends at **4.0** miles at a "diverse" campsite.

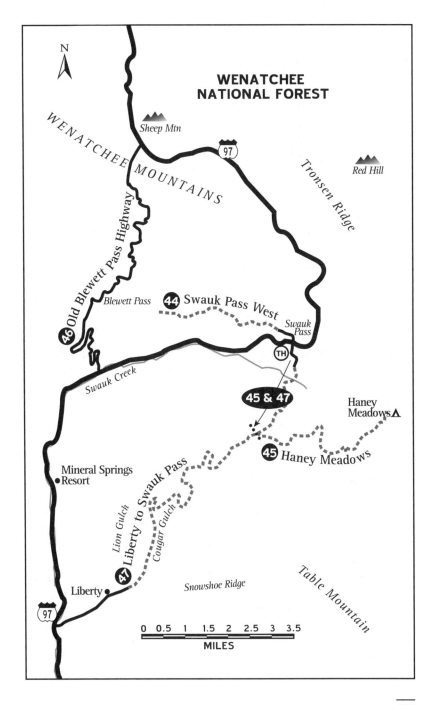

45. Haney Meadows

RATING	⊕⊕⊕⊕
DISTANCE	8.2 miles
ROAD SURFACE	Graded gravel
ROAD CONDITION	Good/Poor
ROAD GRADE	Steep/Extremely steep
PUCKER FACTOR	White knuckles
ACCESSIBLE	Summer, fall
LAND MANAGER/CONTACT	Wenatchee National Forest, Cle Elum Ranger District, (509) 852-1100, www.fs.usda.gov/okawen
TRAILHEADS	Swauk Interpretive
CAMPGROUNDS	Haney Meadows
NOTES	Northwest Forest Pass ($5 daily, $30 annually) required

The Drive

If you're up for the bumpy, rocky, steep final few miles to Haney Meadows, this road is a great adventure to a high mountain grassland ringed by alpine forestland.

Getting There

From Highway 97 at Swauk Pass, turn east into the wide parking area and Sno-Park and drive uphill to the beginning of Forest Road 9716. (See map on page 137.) GPS location: N47°20.109'; W121°34.846'

The Road

Every winter for the past two decades, a bunch of crazy cross-country skiers gather for a noncompetitive cross-country ski adventure called the "Hog Loppet," which I am told means something like "High Lope" in Swedish. It begins at the Mission Ridge wintersports area and ends, 21.0 miles later, at Swauk Pass. The route passes by Haney Meadows and descends to Swauk Pass on Forest Road 9716, the road you'll be traveling on this drive. I can say with certainty that it is just as fun to ski the road as it is to drive it.

And it is more fun to ski it than ride a mountain bike on it, especially if you get a flat tire 5.0 miles from the car and your pump doesn't work, so you have to push your bike downhill the entire distance. But that's another story.

Starting at the Swauk Pass Sno-Park, follow the road as it turns and climbs uphill on broken pavement to round a corner and pass a wide parking area

Haney Meadows are popular both in summer with hikers and in winter with cross-country skiers.

and restroom on the right. A short interpretive trail begins on the east side of the road and makes an interesting loop trip. Beyond, the gravel road is smooth and wide and climbs gently through forest and meadow, with valley views on either side of Swauk Pass. Watch for wildlife along this section; I've seen coyotes trotting along the road and deer galloping in the meadows.

At **3.7** miles, you'll reach a junction with Forest Road 9711, which climbs up from the mining community of Liberty (drive #47). Turn left here, and follow FR 9716 as it climbs, bordered by wildflowers in the summer, eventually rounding a corner to an impressive sight: the jumbled sharp boulders of the west face of Diamond Head, **4.3** miles from Swauk Pass.

This is where the road gets rough. It begins angling steeply up the rocky headwall, where it might be a good idea to look to the top and see if any Hummers are headed in your direction. This lumpy, exposed climb is about 0.7 mile long and reaches a forested pass and junction with Forest Road 35, which crosses Table Mountain and in 27.0 miles, descends to Ellensburg.

You'll keep left and descend a steep open meadow at **5.3** miles, where the road deteriorates to a series of sharp rocks and ruts best suited for vehicles with high ground clearance. Drivers in passenger vehicles should be encouraged to know that I drove the road in a front-wheel-drive compact, and met two women out for a drive in their subcompact sedan. Just take your time and all will be fine.

The road continues downhill for about 1.0 mile, alternately passing meadow and forest, before entering an alpine forest where the road improves slightly. It winds up and down in the woods for about 2.0 miles before arriving at a junction with a short road leading to Haney Meadows Campground and at **8.2** miles, emerging into the open grassland of the meadows at the site of an old forest cabin. It was this same cabin where, the last time I skied in the Hog Loppet, I spent the better part of an hour working to get the knots out of a pair of cramped legs before skiing the final 8.2 miles to Swauk Pass. The beauty of Haney Meadows is worth the trip either way, on skis or in a car.

46. Old Blewett Pass Highway

RATING	⊛⊛⊛
DISTANCE	9.8 miles
ROAD SURFACE	Paved
ROAD CONDITION	Fair
ROAD GRADE	Steep
PUCKER FACTOR	Sightseeing OK
ACCESSIBLE	Summer
LAND MANAGER/CONTACT	Wenatchee National Forest, Cle Elum Ranger District, (509) 852-1100, www.fs.usda.gov/okawen
NOTES	Watch for wildlife

The Drive

Here's a quiet, unrushed way to get over the original Blewett Pass, now called the Old Blewett Pass.

Getting There

From Mineral Springs, follow Highway 97 for 3 miles north to the Old Blewett Pass Highway and turn west. (See map on page 137.) GPS location: N47°19.524'; W120°40.398'

The Road

Now, don't let me confuse you: Swauk Pass is officially Blewett Pass, even though it was originally named Swauk Pass when the new Highway 97 corridor was realigned in 1956. Many people refused to call it Swauk Pass, so the state Department of Transportation changed the name to Blewett Pass. Then, they had to come up with a name for the real Blewett Pass, which was about 5.0 miles west of Swauk Pass—and as you may recall—was renamed Blewett Pass. So they named the real Blewett Pass Old Blewett Pass and the old Highway 97 the Old Blewett Pass Highway.

Never mind all of that. The Old Blewett Pass Highway follows an old wagon road that was carved out of the mountainsides of Swauk Creek by the Blewett Mining Company in the 1900s. It's a nice way to slow down and enjoy the view as you drive over the 4,061-foot summit of, uh, Old Blewett Pass.

From the junction with Highway 97, the road climbs **0.4** mile, then turns right on pavement and begins climbing in open forest, gaining elevation in switchbacks for about 3.0 miles before arriving at a tight hairpin and climbing

Views from the Old Blewett Pass Highway to the north include the Wenatchee Valley.

open meadow slopes with great views down the Swauk River valley to the summit of the pass, **4.0** miles from the highway.

The road now begins to drop in a series of sharp curves into the Peshastin Creek basin, with occasional views to the north of the valley. Continue another 3.0 miles to the confluence of Scotty and Peshastin Creeks, at **7.7** miles, then traverse down to rejoin Highway 97. It's **9.8** miles from where you left the highway, and you can return the way you came, or you can turn right on Highway 97 and drive over Swauk, um, new Blewett Pass.

47. Liberty to Swauk Pass

RATING	❀❀❀❀
DISTANCE	14.0 miles
ROAD SURFACE	Paved/Graded gravel
ROAD CONDITION	Good
ROAD GRADE	Steep
PUCKER FACTOR	Sightseeing OK
ACCESSIBLE	Summer, fall
LAND MANAGER/CONTACT	Wenatchee National Forest, Cle Elum Ranger District, (509) 852-1100, www.fs.usda.gov/okawen
TRAILHEADS	Swauk Interpretive
NOTES	Great views of Central Cascades, Mount Rainier

The Drive

Visit one of the historic mining "ghost towns" of Washington, then continue to climb through open pine forest to alpine country near Swauk Pass.

Getting There

From I-90 at Cle Elum, take exit 85 and follow Highway 970 for 12 miles east to Highway 97, then follow Highway 97 north for 4 miles to a junction with a road leading east to Liberty. Turn right here. (See map on page 137.) GPS location: N47°14.582'; W120°41.839'

The Road

Crystalline gold found in Swauk Creek drew the first residents of Liberty, known originally as Williams Creek, in 1873. Miners still work their claims in the area, but rock climbers and all-terrain vehicle (ATV) pilots in the summer and snowmobilers, snowshoers, and cross-country skiers in the winter also frequent the mountains around Liberty.

Follow the Liberty road for **1.5** miles, passing a junction with Forest Road 9712 on the left. You'll enter the old townsite of Liberty at **1.7** miles, where an interpretive sign outlines the history of the town. In recent years, westside residents have discovered a new kind of gold in Liberty, called "sunshine." As a result, the old town appears to be coming back to life.

Once you've soaked up the history and as much of that new gold as you want, continue east through the town and the end of the paved road at **2.5** miles. Here, you'll find a junction with Forest Road 9718, and you'll stay

Liberty is the oldest mining townsite in the state.

left. A sign here indicates Haney Meadows is 14.0 miles and Lion Rock, 15.0 miles. Stay left again at **2.8** miles, the junction with the Williams Creek Road.

Beyond, the road begins to climb and the view through the forest opens. Stay right at **3.6** miles where an ATV trail (4332) leaves the road. At about **4.0** miles, you'll get a peek across the forest on one of the thumb rocks that attract climbers to their "fun in the sun." You'll enter the high country after a few corners and switchbacks. At **6.0** miles from Highway 97, round a corner above a spectacular overlook and rock pinnacles that plunge into the Swauk Creek drainage to the south.

The route continues to climb along steep hillside and at about **7.0** miles, you'll see the top of Mount Rainier rise to the west. In another 0.2 mile, arrive at a Y junction with Forest Road 9712. This piney plateau serves up spectacular views of the Central Cascade peaks west of Leavenworth. A sign at the junction points to Haney Meadows, 9.0 miles, and Lion Rock, 10.0 miles. Turn right and follow FR 9712, which gets a bit rough, but the view of Rainier is likely to make the bumps and washboarding worthwhile. Lupine and other alpine wildflowers begin to show along the roadside.

At **9.8** miles from your starting point, you'll stay left at a junction with Forest Road 9711, where a sign indicates Haney Meadows is now 6.0 miles, Lion Rock, 7.0 miles. Continue another 0.2 mile to a junction with Forest Road 9716 and turn left. This road descends through pine forest and joins Highway 97 at the summit of Swauk Pass. If you've time, stop at the big parking area and restrooms just before joining Highway 97, where you'll find an easy interpretive loop trail.

I-90 CORRIDOR

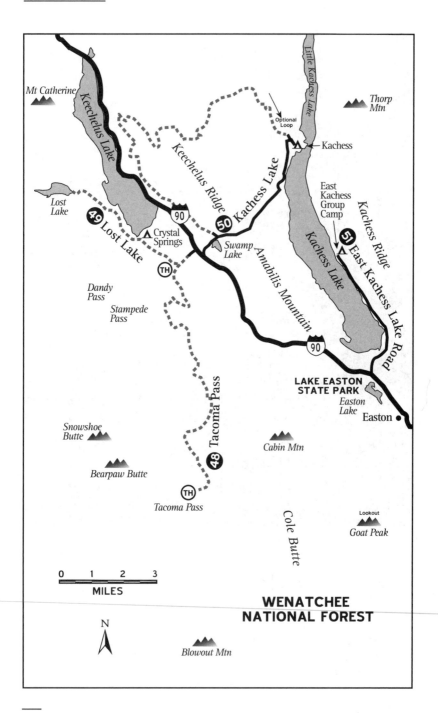

48. Tacoma Pass

RATING	⊛⊛
DISTANCE	12.1 miles
ROAD SURFACE	Paved/Graded gravel
ROAD CONDITION	Good
ROAD GRADE	Moderate
PUCKER FACTOR	Flatlanders welcome
ACCESSIBLE	Summer
LAND MANAGER/CONTACT	Mount Baker–Snoqualmie National Forest, Skykomish Ranger District, (360) 677-2414, www.fs.fed.us/mbs
TRAILHEADS	Pacific Crest
CAMPGROUNDS	Crystal Springs
NOTES	Dusty road

The Drive

This road climbs high above the infant Yakima River to a 3,400-foot pass and junction with the Pacific Crest Trail.

Getting There

Take exit 62 from I-90 and turn west, following the signs to Stampede Pass. GPS location at eastbound junction with Stampede Pass Road: N47°18.291'; W121°18.424'

The Road

The road makes an interesting drive because it follows the transition between the demands of the city to the west and the wide countryside to the east. You'll pass through young and second-growth forestland, underneath utility lines, and past staging areas where gravel and rock supplies were trucked down to the I-90 and railroad corridor below.

Begin by turning west at the freeway exit and passing the entrance to the Crystal Springs Campground, 0.4 mile from the junction. This campground was closed in the summer of 2011 and if you're planning a stop there, make certain you call ahead to see if it's reopened.

The road turns past the campground and crosses the Yakima River before arriving at a junction with a road leading to Lost Lake (drive #49). Stay left and begin climbing toward Stampede Pass on Forest Road 54, switching back under power lines and winding through mostly logged forestland with

Trees line the forest road to Tacoma Pass.

excellent views down to the I-90 corridor and across to the Cascade peaks above Lake Kachess and the Alpine Lakes Wilderness to the northeast.

At **3.3** miles, turn left onto the Tacoma Pass Road, Forest Road 41, as it climbs in second-growth forest to the south. The pavement ends here, but the road is wide and in good condition. You'll pass under power lines where the views down the valley are enhanced by the lack of forest cover, and at about **6.0** miles from the junction, round a hillside below a number of cell and radio towers. The way continues to climb alternately through forest and logged areas and at **10.0** miles, crosses the Cabin Creek drainage and switches back to the left. Just beyond, stay right at the Y intersection with the Cabin Creek Road, Forest Road 52, and at **12.1** miles, arrive at Tacoma Pass, where you'll find the Pacific Crest Trail crossing the road.

If you wish to return to I-90 via a different road, turn around and drive 1.1 miles to the junction with the Cabin Creek Road, FR 52, and turn right. It's 9.7 miles to the junction with I-90 at Easton.

49. Lost Lake

RATING	✪✪✪✪
DISTANCE	5.9 miles
ROAD SURFACE	Paved/Graded gravel
ROAD CONDITION	Good
ROAD GRADE	Steep
PUCKER FACTOR	Sightseeing OK
ACCESSIBLE	Summer
LAND MANAGER/CONTACT	Mount Baker–Snoqualmie National Forest, Skykomish Ranger District, (360) 677-2414, www.fs.fed.us/mbs
TRAILHEADS	John Wayne
CAMPGROUNDS	Crystal Springs
NOTES	Northwest Forest Pass ($5 daily, $30 annually) required

The Drive

Here's a quick, quiet lakeside getaway from the frantic pace of I-90, a good picnic spot when you're heading east or west along the freeway.

Getting There

Take exit 62 from I-90 and turn west, following the signs to Stampede Pass. (See map on page 146.) GPS location at eastbound junction with Stampede Pass Road: N47°18.291'; W121°18.424'

The Road

Lost Lake is a mile-long mountain lake about 3.0 miles as the crow flies from I-90 west of Keechelus Lake, visited mostly by anglers and local residents who don't want to or can't hike to higher Cascade lakes. It's not wilderness, but it's about as close as you can get by driving a car.

Begin by turning west at the freeway exit and passing the entrance to the Crystal Springs Campground, **0.4** mile from the junction. This campground was closed in the summer of 2011 and if you're planning a stop there, make certain you call ahead to see if it's reopened.

The road turns past the campground and crosses the Yakima River before arriving at a junction with the Lost Lake Road, **1.3** miles from the I-90 exit. Turn right here onto the gravel road, where a sign indicates Lost Lake is 4.0 miles and Stampede Pass, to the left, is also 4.0 miles. The road parallels a portion of the John Wayne bicycle trail, just above on the left, for about 1.0

An angler waits for a bite at Lost Lake.

mile, then turns and crosses the trail at **2.6** miles. Stay right at the next road junction and drive another 1.6 miles before turning uphill at Roaring Creek, **4.4** miles from I-90.

You'll pass Lakeview, a private community above the shores of Keechelus Lake, at **4.5** miles and continue climbing on the steepest portion of the road to the west, arriving at a road junction **5.6** miles from the freeway. Turn right here, where a sign indicates Lost Lake is 0.25 mile, and follow the road to the lake access at its eastern end. Turn left to the limited parking area and small boat launch, the best spot for a picnic. The road down to the boat launch is very steep and care should be taken not to high-center when entering or leaving the parking area.

50. Kachess Lake

RATING	❸❸❸
DISTANCE	5.4 miles
ROAD SURFACE	Paved
ROAD CONDITION	Excellent
ROAD GRADE	Flat
PUCKER FACTOR	Flatlanders welcome
ACCESSIBLE	Spring–fall
LAND MANAGER/CONTACT	Okanogan-Wenatchee National Forest, Cle Elum Ranger District, (509) 674-3800, www.fs.usda.gov/okawen
CAMPGROUNDS	Kachess
NOTES	$7 day-use fee at Kachess Campground and Picnic Area

The Drive

Take the short drive from I-90 to a big mountain lake and campground on the sunny side (barely) of the state, with an optional longer and much steeper return to the interstate.

Getting There

Follow I-90 to exit 62 and turn east, following the signs to Kachess Campground. (See map on page 146.) GPS location: N47°18.291'; W121°18.424'

The Road

Kachess Lake couldn't be described as a real retreat from civilization, but it is a good place to enjoy the great outdoors without driving great distances or bouncing along rough roads. Expect company on this outing—but expect to enjoy your adventure as well.

From I-90, the road heads east past Swamp Lake—which, as you might surmise, is a good breeding ground for mosquitoes and the like—for a short **1.0** mile past a sign announcing that Kachess Campground is 4.0 miles distant to the right. At **3.7** miles, the county road ends, but the pavement continues and you'll find yourself driving along the west shore of Lake Kachess, with views across the lake to forestland and low mountains to the east.

The road winds along the lake, passing several wide pullouts before arriving at a T intersection, **5.4** miles from the freeway. Turn right, here, and drive to the Kachess Campground entrance, where you'll be asked to pay

Kachess Campground is popular with watercraft riders and boaters.

a $7 day-use entry fee. A pretty lakeside picnic area is located to the right beyond the fee booth.

For a longer drive, turn left at the T intersection and follow the Forest Road 4930 for 0.5 mile to its junction with Forest Road 4948. This gravel road climbs steeply up and over Keechelus Ridge, to the west, then drops equally steeply to join the Resort Road **9.2** miles from the junction. From the Resort Road junction, you can turn right to the Gold Creek Sno-Park at I-90; or left, to the junction with the road to Kachess Campground at Swamp Lake. Total distance back to I-90 from either road is about 14.0 miles.

51. East Kachess Lake Road

RATING	⚙
DISTANCE	4.8 miles
ROAD SURFACE	Paved/Graded gravel
ROAD CONDITION	Good/Poor
ROAD GRADE	Flat
PUCKER FACTOR	Flatlanders welcome
ACCESSIBLE	Spring–fall
LAND MANAGER/CONTACT	Okanogan-Wenatchee National Forest, Cle Elum Ranger District, (509) 674-3800, www.fs.usda.gov/okawen
CAMPGROUNDS	East Kachess Group
NOTES	Visit on a weekday

The Drive

This is a good road to take if you're short on time and looking for a spot by a lake for a quick picnic.

Getting There

From I-90, take Sparks Road exit 70 and turn north. (See map on page 146.) GPS location: N47°15.022'; W121°11.318'

The Road

This drive leads to the East Kachess Group Campground, used by scouting groups for summer camping and weekend outings, but on weekdays, you may have the picnic shelter and facilities all to yourself. Best bet: Call ahead to the Cle Elum Ranger District to see if anyone is occupying the campground.

Begin by passing the Kachess Dam Road in **0.2** mile, and stay right on Forest Road 4818, where the pavement ends. Drive through dense forest above the east shore of the lake and watch for wildlife along this relatively unpopulated stretch of road. You'll pass a junction with an unsigned road leading uphill to the right at **2.9** miles; keep left.

Beyond, you'll get peekaboo views of the lake through the forest and where clearings have been cut for private homes. You'll arrive at a spring and a road junction signed Kachess Lane at **4.3** miles, where the road deteriorates, becoming a series of lumpy rocks where it's wise to drive very slowly. At **4.8** miles, you'll find a wide parking area and a gated road leading down to the campground. You can park here and walk down to the shelter or follow several pathways down to the lake. Sitting along the shore depends upon

The group campground on the east side of Kachess Lake looks across at the crowded side of the lake.

the lake level; during a visit in July, the lake was too high to get to the shore, but the bank above made a good spot to sit and watch the crowds at Kachess Campground on the opposite shore.

You can continue another 1.7 miles on the road, which stays as rough as the previous 0.5 mile. Access to the lake is limited.

52. Tucquala Meadows

RATING	⚙️⚙️⚙️⚙️⚙️
DISTANCE	28.9 miles
ROAD SURFACE	Paved/Graded gravel
ROAD CONDITION	Good/Fair
ROAD GRADE	Steep
PUCKER FACTOR	Sightseeing OK
ACCESSIBLE	Summer, fall
LAND MANAGER/CONTACT	Okanogan-Wenatchee National Forest, Cle Elum Ranger District, (509) 674-3800, www.fs.usda.gov/okawen
TRAILHEADS	Sasse Mountain, Jolly Mountain Lookout, Davis Peak Lookout, Squaw Lake, Deception Pass
CAMPGROUNDS	Wish Poosh, Cle Elum River, Salmon La Sac, Red Mountain, Scatter Creek
NOTES	Northwest Forest Pass ($5 daily, $30 annually) required

The Drive

Here's a rough and sometimes dusty road that is well worth the ride and car wash when you get home. It passes a beautiful lake, follows a crystal river upstream, and ends in alpine meadows huddled between the Cascade peaks of the Alpine Lakes Wilderness.

Getting There

Take exit 80 off I-90 and drive northeast on Bullfrog Road for 2.8 miles to the Salmon La Sac Road, Highway 903. Turn left on Highway 903, passing the Roslyn Rodeo Grounds, on the right. GPS location: N47°12.657'; W120°59.035'

The Road

This drive has something for just about everyone. First, you'll drive through a couple of historic mining towns where the old television series *Northern Exposure* was filmed. Then you'll pass a big lake where there's waterside camping or, if you prefer, more luxurious digs. Next, you'll drive up a river where you'll find dozens of camping or picnic spots.

But the best is yet to come. Turn uphill beside the crashing Cle Elum River and climb into a steep-walled mountain valley, drive across creeks, and arrive

Cathedral Rock is reflected in ponds at Tucquala Meadows.

at a mountain meadow trailhead underneath an iconic Cascade peak. All this, and you're on the sunny side of the state.

Follow Highway 903 through Roslyn, known in the television series as Cicely, Alaska, and the smaller mining village of Ronald before starting downhill at Lakedale to the eastern shore of Lake Cle Elum. At **7.6** miles, you'll pass a road leading to Wish Poosh Campground, the first camping opportunity on the lake. The lake comes into view around **9.0** miles from Roslyn, and you'll follow the lakeshore for about 4.0 miles to the Cle Elum River Campground, **13.1** miles from Roslyn. A bridge crosses the river here and heads up French Cabin Creek and you'll see a sign indicating mileages to Salmon La Sac Campground, Cooper Lake, and Tucquala Lake. Stay right and continue on Highway 903.

At **14.**2 miles, pass the Red Mountain Campground entrance, and continue on the highway to a junction with the Cooper Lake Road (drive #53), **15.6** miles from Roslyn. Stay right and drive another 1.0 mile to the junction with Forest Road 4330.

Turn right onto the gravel FR 4330 and climb steeply above the Cle Elum River. Expect to encounter sections of severely washboarded road, especially around corners. The view opens up as you climb, passing rustic cabins by the river and on the slopes above. Round China Point at **16.6** miles, and stay left at **18.8** miles, where a spur road climbs uphill to private summer cabins.

As you climb higher, you'll begin to see a change in the forest. The pines of the dry lower forest begin to share their canopy with fir and cedar, and the slopes of the mountains above begin to put on an evergreen cloak. The road levels somewhat from the steep initial hills and the Cle Elum River, off to the left, slows its rush to the lake. You'll drive into and across Scatter Creek and in about 0.5 mile, arrive at Tucquala Lake. The water level in this lake fluctuates from year to year and season to season.

Beyond, you'll pass the Fish Lake Guard Station in a high meadow, **26.8** miles from Roslyn, then bump along the road for another 2.0 miles, arriving at the end of the road and the Squaw Lake and Deception Pass trailheads, where you'll find a large parking area, campsites, and a restroom. The meadows here are filled with both wildflowers and bugs in midsummer and are almost as colorful in the fall, after a frost has reduced the bug population.

A short, easy walk on the Squaw Lake Trail leads to a bridge across the infant Cle Elum River, with views up- and downstream. Mountains scratch clouds above, and the prominent rock peak to the northwest is 6,724-foot Cathedral Rock. Snowfields stretch beyond at Deception Pass along the Pacific Crest Trail.

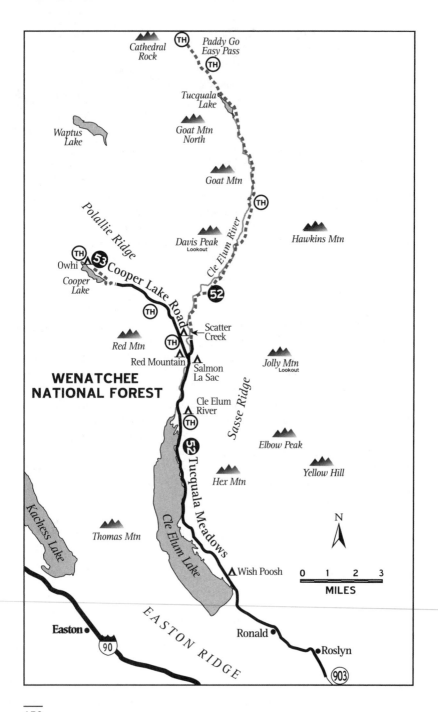

53. Cooper Lake Road

RATING	⊛⊛⊛⊛⊛
DISTANCE	5.7 miles
ROAD SURFACE	Paved/Graded gravel
ROAD CONDITION	Good
ROAD GRADE	Steep
PUCKER FACTOR	Flatlanders welcome
ACCESSIBLE	Summer, fall
LAND MANAGER/CONTACT	Wenatchee National Forest, Cle Elum Ranger District, (509) 852-1100, www.fs.fed.us/r6/wenatchee
TRAILHEADS	Red Mountain, Mineral Creek, Pete Lake
CAMPGROUNDS	Owhi
NOTES	Northwest Forest Pass ($5 daily, $30 annually) required at Cooper Lake

The Drive

The road to Cooper Lake leads to one of the nicest walk-in tent campgrounds in the state and a great day-trip destination for picnickers.

Getting There

From the roundabout in Roslyn, follow the Salmon La Sac Road, Highway 903, north for 15.6 miles (for a road description, see drive #52, Salmon La Sac to Tucquala Meadows) to the Cle Elum River bridge. Turn right and cross the Cle Elum River on the Cooper Lake Road. (See map on page 158.) GPS location: N47°23.078'; W121°05.648'

The Road

I first visited Cooper Lake more than a decade ago, paddling my old canoe, the Leaky Tiki, on its mirror waters and testing my angling prowess by dragging Power Bait around on a hook. As those of you who have used Power Bait know, there really isn't much angling prowess involved in catching the wily trout.

The lake is nestled in a deep forest basin that blocks views of the big mountains around it. What makes the area so spectacular is the view west from the lakeshore. You'll look up the lake to the snowcapped glory of the Alpine Lakes Wilderness. If you've a canoe or kayak, it's only a short carry from the parking area above the Owhi Campground to the lakeshore. The lake isn't particularly large and you can paddle from one end to the other in less

Cooper River meanders through forest at Cooper Lake.

than 30 minutes, but you'll undoubtedly want to take more time than that to admire the view.

The paved road begins climbing immediately after crossing the Cle Elum River, passing the Red Mountain trailhead **1.6** miles from the bridge. The road continues to climb and though paved, you'll want to keep your eye out for frost heaves and several healthy chuckholes. At **3.6** miles, you'll pass a junction with Forest Road 4613 and continue to the right.

The pavement ends at **4.8** miles, at a junction with a forest road climbing to the Mineral Creek trailhead. Turn right here and pass a number of driveways to private residences on the left, crossing Cooper Creek in 0.2 mile. Across the bridge, follow the road as it turns left and bumps into the Owhi Campground parking area, where you'll find restrooms and trails leading down to the lake. The road past Owhi Campground leads another 1.0 mile to the Pete Lake trailhead, but unless you're looking for a hike, Owhi is the place for you.

54. Taneum Creek Road

RATING	✿✿✿
DISTANCE	15.0 miles
ROAD SURFACE	Paved
ROAD CONDITION	Good
ROAD GRADE	Moderate
PUCKER FACTOR	Flatlanders welcome
ACCESSIBLE	Year-round
LAND MANAGER/CONTACT	Okanogan-Wenatchee National Forest, Cle Elum Ranger District, (509) 674-3800, www.fs.usda.gov/okawen
CAMPGROUNDS	Taneum, Taneum Meadows, Icewater, Taneum Junction
NOTES	Northwest Forest Pass ($5 daily, $30 annually) required

The Drive

Here's an easy drive along a pine tree–lined creek and basalt canyon to a campground and picnic spot by the water.

Getting There

If you're eastbound on I-90, take exit 93 and turn left across the Interstate. Westbound traffic: turn right at exit. GPS location: N47°06.839'; W120°47.518'

The Road

I might have given this road a better recommendation, except that thieves stole my sleeping bag and pad out of my tent at Taneum Campground while I was out driving wild roads. I arrived at the campground in late evening to be confronted with a choice of sleeping on the cold, hard ground like a dog or retreating to an Ellensburg motel. I packed up my tent—still haven't figured out why they didn't take it, too—and retreated to a motel.

But don't let my sad tale keep you from driving the Taneum Creek Road (local residents pronounce it "TANE-um"). It's a pleasant, scenic road. Begin by turning south on the Thorp Prairie Road, **0.4** mile from the I-90 interchange. This paved road passes a fruit stand and parallels the interstate, then winds down Rocky Canyon to a junction with the East Taneum Road, **3.9** miles from the interchange. Turn right and cross the interstate to a junction with the West Taneum Road. Turn right here, and follow the West Taneum Road as it enters the Taneum Creek valley.

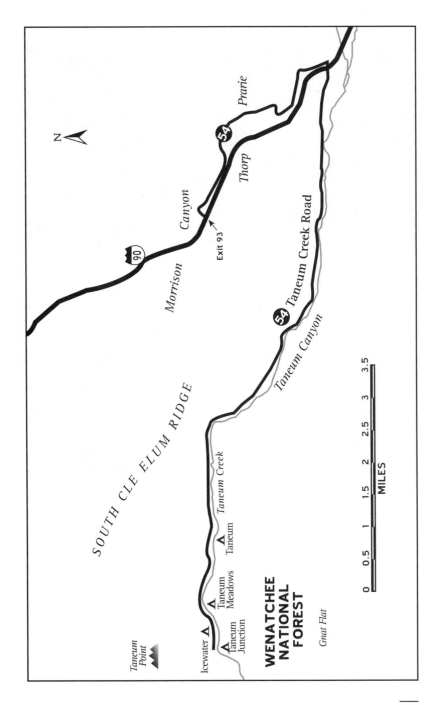

N

Prarie

54

Thorp

Canyon

Morrison

Exit 93

90

Taneum Creek Road

54 Taneum Creek Road

Taneum Canyon

SOUTH CLE ELUM RIDGE

Taneum Creek

Taneum

Taneum Meadows

Icewater

Taneum Junction

Taneum Point

WENATCHEE NATIONAL FOREST

Gnat Flat

0   0.5   1   1.5   2   2.5   3   3.5

MILES

Campers drive across Taneum Creek to get to Taneum Campground.

Farms line the valley flats to the left, while the brown hillsides of the L. T. Murray Wildlife Area rise on your right. You'll pass farmhouses and at **6.2** miles, leave the farms behind and wind under big basalt cliffs by the creek. Cross into the Okanogan-Wenatchee National Forest at **9.6** miles, where Taneum Creek reduced the road to one lane at a washout and the thoroughfare gains the designation Forest Road 33. At **10.7** miles, FR 33 passes Taneum Campground, where the road is closed at Sno-Park areas in the winter.

The campground is located in giant pines along the creek and you'll find a nice day-use area at the water's edge. To get to the campground, ford Taneum Creek on a concrete ramp.

Back on FR 33, you'll climb along the creek, passing Taneum Meadows Campground at **11.0** miles and Icewater Campground on the left, **13.3** miles. You'll find roads leading to Buck Meadows and Quartz Mountain; both roads were closed in the summer of 2011. Stay right at **13.5** miles and drive another 1.4 miles to the Taneum Junction Campground, a good picnic and turnaround point.

It is possible to follow FR 33 and its spur roads for at least 10.0 more miles and even take wild roads through the forest to Cle Elum. But the scenery doesn't get any better, and you pass a number of clear-cut mountainsides along the way.

55. Yakima Canyon Road

RATING	⊛⊛⊛⊛
DISTANCE	25.4 miles
ROAD SURFACE	Paved
ROAD CONDITION	Excellent
ROAD GRADE	Moderate
PUCKER FACTOR	Flatlanders welcome
ACCESSIBLE	Year-round
LAND MANAGER/CONTACT	Bureau of Land Management, Spokane District, (509) 665-2100, www.blm.gov/or/districts/spokane
TRAILHEADS	Umtanum Canyon
CAMPGROUNDS	Bighorn, Umtanum, Lmuma, Big Pines, Roza
NOTES	$5 day-use fee, May 15–Sept. 15

The Drive

One of the most scenic drives in the state follows the Yakima River canyon for more than 24 miles, with picnic areas, campgrounds, and hiking trails along a world-class trout fishery.

Getting There

From I-90, take exit 109 and turn south on the Yakima Canyon Road, then drive to the canyon entrance at Thrall Road. GPS location: N46°55.583'; W120°30.616'

The Road

Many motorists, including me, choose the Yakima River Road, Highway 821, as an alternate to Interstate 82 in getting from Ellensburg to Yakima. It's one of those roads you don't want to miss whenever you're around Central Washington.

Though you'd hardly classify it as wild, the Yakima Canyon Road has many of the elements of some national forest roads. It passes through relatively unpopulated areas and the river beside the road is much the same as it was hundreds of thousands of years ago, when it began digging its ditch through a lava field that covered much of Washington, Oregon, and Idaho. You're likely to see deer and perhaps mountain sheep grazing on the hillsides or scrambling up basalt cliffs; reptiles—including rattlesnakes—and raptors also call the canyon home.

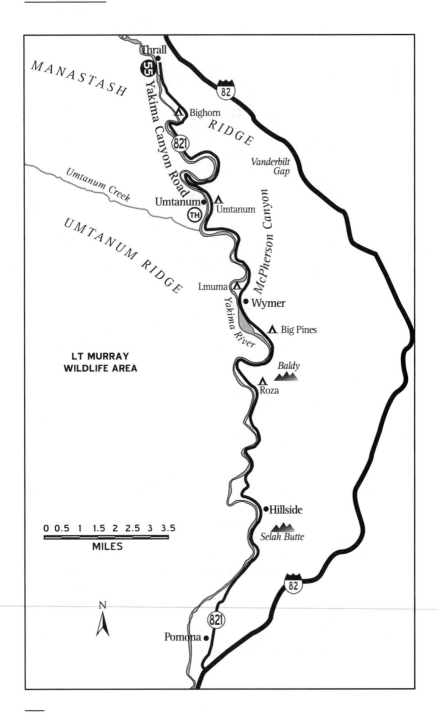

Picnic areas and campsites are found at four BLM sites along the Yakima Canyon.

Note the 45-mile-per-hour speed limit upon passing the Yakima Canyon Entrance, which is enforced with vigor by both Washington State Patrol officers and Kittitas County Sheriff's deputies. The road passes a monument and interpretive sign near the entrance to the canyon before passing the private Bighorn Campground, **3.1** miles from the entrance.

Beyond, you'll pass several farms and private homes above the road and at **8.7** miles, arrive at the Umtanum Recreation Area. This is a good place for a picnic and a chance to explore the river on the other side of the canyon—a footbridge crosses the river here, where a trail strikes west up the barren hills above Umtanum Canyon. Besides the picnic area, several developed campsites are available for $15 per night during the summer.

Canyon River Estates, a posh private development, is **10.4** miles from the canyon entrance, once the site of a fishing resort and campground. Just beyond, the road climbs the hillside away from the river, snakes through a side canyon, and drops back to river level, passing a heritage marker at **12.6** miles, the entrance to Lmuma Creek Recreation Site, one of the newer sites developed by the Bureau of Land Management. You'll find campsites and picnic areas at Lmuma Creek.

One of the several fishing access areas for river anglers is located at **15.2** miles. Trophy catch-and-release fishing for rainbow trout attracts fly fishers from throughout the state and beyond. They cast from shore or float in riverboats with guides from Yakima or Ellensburg.

Big Pines Recreation Site is next, **15.6** miles from the canyon entrance. It's the largest and most recently developed of the BLM sites in the canyon, with campsites, a picnic area, restrooms, and a boat launch. In another 2.5 miles, arrive at Roza Recreation Site, another nice facility with camping, picnicking, and restrooms.

Beyond Roza, the road climbs above the Roza Dam, **18.4** miles, and leaves the end of the canyon drive **23.1** miles from the entrance. Continue another 1.7 miles south to an interchange with I-82, which can be followed to Yakima or Ellensburg. Me? I'd turn around and drive back down the canyon.

Because of low traffic volumes and decreased auto speeds, the Canyon Road is a favorite with some bicyclists, especially for the "Your Canyon for a Day" bike tour. It usually takes place on a Sunday in May when the sponsors, Yakima County Crime Stoppers, close the road for about six hours to auto traffic, and bicyclists have it all to themselves.

HIGHWAY 410

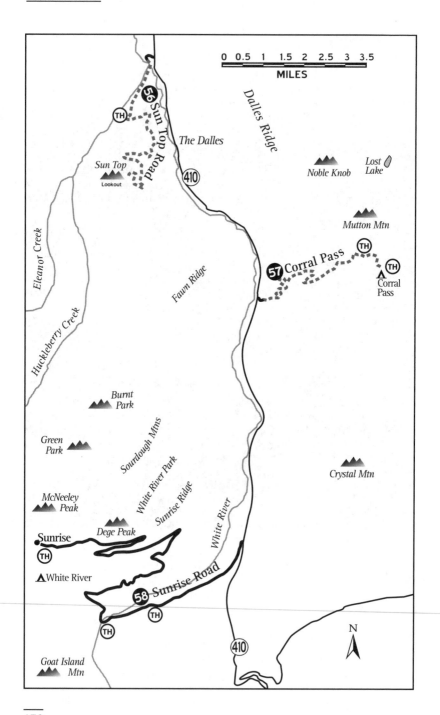

56. Sun Top Road

RATING	❂❂❂❂❂
DISTANCE	6.8 miles
ROAD SURFACE	Graded gravel/Graded dirt
ROAD CONDITION	Fair
ROAD GRADE	Steep
PUCKER FACTOR	White knuckles
ACCESSIBLE	Summer, fall
LAND MANAGER/CONTACT	Mount Baker–Snoqualmie National Forest, Enumclaw office, (360) 825-6585, www.fs.fed.us/mbs
TRAILHEADS	Sun Top
NOTES	Best driven on bluebird days

The Drive

The road leading to the old Forest Service fire lookout is dusty and bumpy, but the view of Mount Rainier and beyond makes it an excellent day trip.

Getting There

Follow Chinook Pass Highway 410 southeast from Enumclaw to Forest Road 73, just past milepost 49. Turn right and drive 1.8 miles to a junction with Forest Road 7315, the Sun Top Road, and stay left on Forest Road 7315. GPS location: N47°04.327'; W121°34.993'

The Road

Sun Top Lookout, a 5,270-foot-high fire lookout, makes a great spot for a picnic, an exhilarating ride for a mountain biker, or a challenging climb for a hiker. The dirt and gravel road to the summit is the easiest way to get there, and you'll likely find a friendly volunteer to show you around.

But you won't need any help locating Mount Rainier on a clear day. It's so close that with binoculars, you can watch climbers wind their way through crevasse fields on the mountain.

Volunteers from the communities of Greenwater and Enumclaw get together every spring to join a drawing for a chance to stay overnight at the lookout. Built in the mid-1930s, the lookout is on the National Register of Historic Places. It's a ground-level lookout, so there's no scrambling up an airy staircase—but there is a short, steep trail from the parking area to the lookout itself.

Bill Steel, a volunteer at the Sun Top Lookout, gets a good view of Mount Rainier.

You'll find a picnic table with a grand view of Rainier and the White River and Huckleberry Creek basins, 3,000 feet below. Crystal Mountain and the Cascades are to the east, and far across the horizon to the west are the Olympic Mountains.

The road switches back up Sun Top Mountain, changing from deep forest to alpine country as it reaches the top. The last 0.5 mile of the single-lane road is along an airy, steep mountainside, but there's a wide parking area for turning around, just below the trail to the lookout.

57. Corral Pass

RATING	✪✪✪✪
DISTANCE	5.5 miles
ROAD SURFACE	Graded gravel
ROAD CONDITION	Fair
ROAD GRADE	Extremely steep
PUCKER FACTOR	White knuckles
ACCESSIBLE	Summer, fall
LAND MANAGER/CONTACT	Mount Baker–Snoqualmie National Forest, Snoqualmie Ranger District, Enumclaw, (360) 825-6585, www.fs.fed.us/mbs
TRAILHEADS	Rainier View, Greenwater Lakes, Noble Knob
CAMPGROUNDS	Corral Pass
NOTES	Northwest Forest Pass ($5 daily, $30 annually)

The Drive

This is a steep, rough drive to a fantastic view of Mount Rainier and a beautiful tent campground most RVs simply can't reach.

Getting There

From Highway 410 in Enumclaw, drive 31 miles south through Greenwater (watch the speed trap!) to Forest Road 7174 and turn left. (See map on page 170.) GPS location: N46°59.989'; W121°31.721'

The Road

Here's the way the good folks at the Mount Baker–Snoqualmie National Forest describe Corral Pass in their campground guide:

"Corral Pass is located in a beautiful alpine setting with several hiking trails within walking distance. The Rainier View Trail provides scenic overlooks while the Greenwater Lakes Trail accesses the Norse Peak Wilderness. Noble Knob Trail is nearby and open to mountain bikes. The steep, narrow, winding road that accesses the campground is not recommended for trailers or RVs."

They add:

"Very rough and steep road; high-clearance vehicles are recommended. Drive slowly and cautiously over sharp rock beds. Not recommended for inexperienced mountain drivers."

The Corral Pass begins with a steep climb from Highway 410.

I first attempted this road in my four-wheel-drive truck and camper, got about 1.5 miles up the road—to the fifth of a dozen switchbacks—and rounded the hairpin where the 2,200-pound camper's butt dragged on a huge dirt mound in the road. The left front tiedown on the camper broke and it slid about a foot off the pickup bed. I eased the truck up the hill to a wide spot where, after about 16 repetitions of backing up a foot or so, then turning and driving forward a foot or so, I managed to turn the vehicle around.

The next problem I faced was getting the camper back on the truck. You don't just slide a one-ton truck house back where it belongs, you know. So I let gravity do the job. I got going about 5 miles an hour, then jammed on the brakes. The camper slid into place, I put a spare tiedown on, and I (carefully!) got the hell out of there. The next weekend, I returned in the four-wheel-drive SUV and drove up to Corral Pass.

Now, all of this is not meant to frighten you into not driving the Corral Pass Road, although some who've been there are sure to take umbrage at my recommending the road. It is, after all, one of the best tent campgrounds in Washington, 5,651 feet above sea level, and you can't blame them for wanting to keep it all to themselves.

Drivers in two-wheel-drive sedans and subcompact cars can drive the Corral Pass Road without worry if they simply slow down and navigate around the big bumps on the hairpin corners with care. This road is better than the Twin Lakes Road (drive #18) and like that road, I saw two-wheel-drive passenger cars of all sizes at Corral Pass. So hop in and give it a try. The worst that can happen is you'll decide to turn around.

The gravel road passes several cabins as it climbs alongside Goat Creek before making a wide switchback. The forest is thick on either side of the road, so you won't see much as you climb steeply around 10 more switchbacks, all spaced several hundred yards apart. The grade eases a bit at about **3.1** miles, the last switchback, but still climbs for another 1.0 mile, breaking above timberline in sloping meadows about **4.2** miles from the highway. Alpine trees do little to block your view of Mount Rainier across the White River valley, before you round a corner to the east and arrive at a junction with a road leading left to the Noble Knob trailhead, **5.3** miles from the highway.

Keep right, and drive another 0.2 mile over Corral Pass to the campground. The views here are to the east and low peaks to the west block your view of Rainier. No worries. You'll see it on the way down.

58. Sunrise Road

RATING	⊛⊛⊛⊛⊛
DISTANCE	14.8 miles
ROAD SURFACE	Paved
ROAD CONDITION	Excellent
ROAD GRADE	Steep
PUCKER FACTOR	Sightseeing OK
ACCESSIBLE	Summer, fall
LAND MANAGER/CONTACT	Mount Rainier National Park, (360) 569-2211, ext. 1 (recording), www.nps.gov/mora
TRAILHEADS	Owyhigh Lakes, Fryingpan Creek, Sunrise Lake, Sourdough Ridge, Burroughs Mountain, Fremont Lookout
CAMPGROUNDS	White River
NOTES	$15 per carload entry fee at White River Entrance

The Drive

This is the kinder, gentler way to get high on Mount Rainier. Drive to a 6,400-foot-high mountain meadow so close it looks as if you could reach out and touch the Emmons Glacier.

Getting There

Follow Highway 410 through Enumclaw and Greenwater (watch the speed trap!) to Mount Rainier National Park, just south of Crystal Mountain Boulevard. Continue to the junction with the White River Road and turn right. (See map on page 170.) GPS location: N46°54.940'; W121°32.170'

The Road

Sunrise is the second most visited location in Mount Rainier National Park, and with little wonder: besides the 14,411-foot mountain Native Americans called Tahoma, you can see most of the Cascade crest, Mount Adams, and rivers and valleys forever. So expect crowds.

Still, if you get to Sunrise at sunrise or shortly thereafter, you may find all that beauty pretty much for your eyes only. Things don't really get lively around Sunrise until 9 or 10 a.m. on weekends. And don't forget: they named it Sunrise for a reason—morning light hits the mountain like a Saturn rocket.

You needn't go any farther than the Sunrise parking lot to get a view of Mount Rainier.

The road angles downhill through forest, passing a massive avalanche chute, to the White River Entrance Station, where you'll be asked to pay a $15 per carload entry fee. If you're arriving early, you'll find a self-issuing fee box at the entrance booth. Beyond, the road winds along above the White River, where elk are often seen in the autumn. Pass the Owyhigh Lakes trailhead at **3.7** miles and round the curve at the Fryingpan Creek trailhead, **4.4** miles from the highway.

The trail at Fryingpan Creek climbs up to Summerland and beyond, to Panhandle Gap and the Fryingpan Glacier, a good choice for summer skiers as soon as the road opens. You'll climb from here on the road to a junction with a road leading to the White River Campground and trailheads to Glacier Meadows. Mountaineers headed up this side of Rainier usually stage at the White River Campground.

Stay right at this junction and begin the steep climb to Sunrise. The road is two-lane, but lacks shoulders of any size, and bicyclists as well as deer, bears, and other wild critters use the thoroughfare. The road switches back several times in steep canyons where snowdrifts may linger long into July, then reaches the most impressive switchback of all at **13.3** miles. Between the uphill and downhill turn is a big parking area where you can stop and ogle the scenery. Mount Adams can be seen to the south, Crystal Mountain ridge to the east, and the Cascade crest to the north. A trail at this switchback leads steeply downhill to Sunrise Lake, which you can see from the sidewalk on the north side of the road.

The best view of Rainier is yet to come: as you drive under the peaks and sloping green meadows of Sourdough Ridge on the right, Tahoma towers above you like a giant ice sculpture. It glows in the morning sun. Sunrise provides a huge parking area, a snack bar and visitor center, restrooms, and a number of trails. For a 360-degree view, follow the moderately steep trail up to the summit of Sourdough Ridge, about 0.3 mile.

59. Raven Roost

RATING   ♾♾♾♾
DISTANCE   16.7 miles
ROAD SURFACE   Paved/Graded gravel
ROAD CONDITION   Fair
ROAD GRADE   Steep
PUCKER FACTOR   Sightseeing OK
ACCESSIBLE   Summer, fall
LAND MANAGER/CONTACT   Okanogan-Wenatchee National Forest, Naches Ranger District, (509) 653-1401, www.fs.usda.gov/okawen
CAMPGROUNDS   Kaner Flats, Crow Creek, Sand Creek, Huckleberry Forest
NOTES   Road ends with steep, rocky climb

The Drive
Here's a road on the sunshine side of the state that serves up tasty huckleberries and luscious views of Mount Rainier.

Getting There
Follow Highway 410 for 27 miles east of Chinook Pass to its junction with the Little Naches River Road, Forest Road 19, and turn west. GPS location: N46°59.393'; W121°05.784'

The Road
The surprise at the end of this road is the view of 14,411-foot Mount Rainier, which you may have thought you wouldn't see again once you crested Chinook Pass. Yet there is that big vanilla snow cone, courtesy of this 6,168-foot-high bluff, more than 1,500 feet higher than Chinook Pass.

And you've arrived here via a mountain road that follows a clear river, passing a number of pretty forest campgrounds, climbing to a forest so rich with huckleberries there's a campsite named for it. A mountaintop meadow just below the viewpoint makes a good alternate picnic spot to Raven Roost itself, which has a couple of utility towers spiking from the summit.

Begin by following the Little Naches River Road, Forest Road 19, for 2.8 miles to its junction with Forest Road 1902, just beyond Kaner Flats Campground. Turn left on FR 1902 and cross Crow Creek at Crow Creek Campground, 3.2 miles from Highway 410. Turn left at the sign indicating Raven

Mount Rainier from Raven Roost.

Roost is 13.0 miles. The pavement ends in another 0.5 mile, and you begin climbing in a forest of mixed pine, larch, and fir above Crow Creek.

Keep left at an unsigned junction **8.5** miles from Highway 410, crossing Sand Creek about **9.2** miles from the highway and passing nice campsites by the creek. Stay left at an unsigned junction just beyond, **9.7** miles. The road now climbs above Sand Creek to a junction with Forest Road 859. Stay left at this junction, climbing on a rough, rocky road on a lupine-lined lane.

You'll pass junctions with a number of ATV trails about **13.0** miles from Highway 410 and at **14.5** miles, arrive at the Huckleberry Forest Camp, where—as you might gather from the name—you'll find plenty of juicy berries in August and September. Follow bumpy Forest Road 565 as it climbs a hillside to a junction with Forest Road 866 at a meadow, **16.2** miles from the highway.

The final steep 0.5 mile follows FR 866 as it switches back around Raven Roost. This approach is on a rough, rocky road where you'll want to watch for bumps that could be troublesome for sedans with low ground clearance. Once atop the peak, however, there's plenty of room to park and turn around. Big logs line the Rainier overlook, which is a fairly steep west-facing slope.

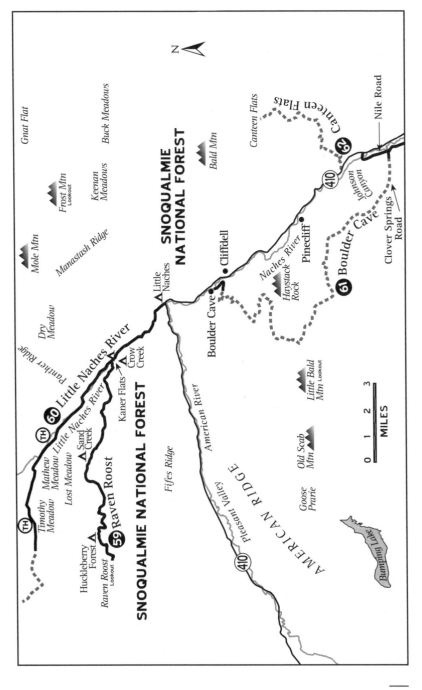

60. Little Naches River

RATING	✹✹✹
DISTANCE	16.1 miles
ROAD SURFACE	Paved/Graded gravel
ROAD CONDITION	Excellent
ROAD GRADE	Moderate
PUCKER FACTOR	Flatlanders welcome
ACCESSIBLE	Spring–fall
LAND MANAGER/CONTACT	Okanogan-Wenatchee National Forest, Naches Ranger District, (509) 653-1401, www.fs.usda.gov/okawen
TRAILHEADS	Pyramid Peak, Naches
CAMPGROUNDS	Little Naches, Kaner Flat
NOTES	Northwest Forest Pass ($5 daily, $30 annually) required

The Drive
Here's a pleasant Sunday drive along a clear stream past campgrounds, picnic areas, and wide meadows where deer and elk roam.

Getting There
Follow Highway 410 for 27 miles east of Chinook Pass to its junction with the Little Naches River Road, Forest Road 19, and turn west. (See map on page 183.) GPS location: N46°59.393'; W121°05.784'

The Road
This beautiful drive is a relaxing mountain getaway for anyone who enjoys the alpine countryside but isn't interested in bumping and thumping along a gravel road. All but the last 2.0 miles of the Little Naches Road, Forest Road 19, is paved—but that shouldn't be taken as an invitation to speed up. Pull over and let the folks racing to the campgrounds and trailhead pass, and enjoy the scenery at a slower pace.

Too many great campgrounds and "diverse" camping areas wait along this road, beginning with the Little Naches Campground on the left at the start of your drive. Sites along the river are distant from Highway 410 and shaded by tall pines.

Beyond, you'll pass a junction with Forest Road 1901 and keep left along the river. Kaner Flat Campground is on the right, 2.3 miles from the highway, and the Pyramid Peak trailhead is 0.4 mile beyond.

Meadows along the Little Naches River.

Next, arrive at a junction with Forest Road 1902, the road to Raven Roost (drive #59), **2.8** miles from the highway. Keep right here, and continue past nice riverside campsites as the road crosses the Little Naches several times. The "diverse" campsite at mile **4.3** might make a good picnic site if it's not occupied.

As the road climbs higher, fir trees begin to populate the forest, which forms a patchwork along the river between neat grassy meadows that look as if they've been tended by a groundskeeper. Look for deer and elk on the edges of the meadows.

You'll pass 4-Way Meadow at mile **7.3**, and the historic Naches Trail **10.2** miles from the highway. The road begins to climb out of the valley at this point and at **12.0** miles, passes a junction with Forest Road 1913. Stay left here, and continue another 2.5 miles to the end of the pavement.

A bumpy gravel road continues past this point, worth exploring for a couple of miles simply to look down on the quiet forest below. The road is lined with purple mountain lupine, a splendid alpine flower with leaf clusters that gather raindrops into shiny pearl-shaped pools.

61. Boulder Cave

RATING	⚙⚙⚙
DISTANCE	22.3 miles
ROAD SURFACE	Paved/Graded gravel
ROAD CONDITION	Good/Fair
ROAD GRADE	Steep
PUCKER FACTOR	Sightseeing OK
ACCESSIBLE	Summer, fall
LAND MANAGER/CONTACT	Okanogan-Wenatchee National Forest, Naches Ranger District, (509) 653-1401, www.fs.usda.gov/okawen
NOTES	Northwest Forest Pass ($5 daily, $30 annually) required

The Drive

This is the long forest route to see a nice picnic area by the Naches River and a trail climbing to a walk through a cave that hosts hibernating bats.

Getting There

Follow Highway 410 for about 39.0 miles east from Chinook Pass to the Nile Loop Road, the detour around the 2009 landslide that destroyed 0.5 mile of Highway 410, and turn right to cross the Naches River on the Nile Loop Road. Follow this road for 1.5 miles to the Clover Springs Road and turn right.

If driving west, turn left at the Nile Loop Road detour at milepost 108 and follow the Nile Loop Road for 3.3 miles to the Clover Springs Road and turn left. (See map on page 183.) GPS location: N46°50.340'; W120°57.081'

Note: The Nile Loop Road has a 35-mile-per-hour speed limit, which is rabidly enforced by friendly Washington State Patrol troopers. You have been warned.

The Road

Now, if you've been paying attention, you would have noticed signs pointing to Boulder Cave about 15.0 miles back on Highway 410. You weren't hallucinating—that was the short route to Boulder Cave, the home of hibernating bats in the winter and a fascinating place to visit. Don't worry, you'll get there after a more relaxing drive through the Okanogan-Wenatchee National Forest.

The Clover Springs Road, Forest Road 1600, passes private homes and farms for **2.0** miles before entering the national forest. Tall fences beside

The entrance to Boulder Cave.

the road are part of the state Department of Fish and Wildlife program to keep elk migrating to the lowlands in the winter away from farm crops and orchards. These splendid animals gather in herds to the east at the Oak Creek Wildlife Area (drive #69), where you can watch volunteers feed them during the winter.

After entering the forest, you'll begin to climb through big pines to a junction with Forest Road 1601 at **3.0** miles. Stay right on FR 1600, where a sign indicates Clover Springs is 16.0 miles. The road passes a second junction at **4.2** miles, where you'll keep left.

You'll drive past some massive pine trees in open forest where it's easy to spot deer and perhaps elk. At **9.0** miles, you'll arrive at a junction with Forest Road 1605, which was closed in the summer of 2011. Continue on FR 1600 and pass Forest Road 1607 at **10.2** miles, keeping left at the junction. Bear right at **12.3** miles, passing a junction with Forest Road 1608, where there's a hunting campsite on the right. Stay right and arrive at a junction with Forest Road 1706 at **12.9** miles, where you'll turn downhill to the right on FR 1706. The roadside along this stretch is lined with mountain lupine; you've climbed above 4,400 feet.

At mile **17.5**, you'll pass a junction with Forest Road 322 and keep right, dropping down to a junction with Forest Road 1709 at **18.1** miles. Stay right and continue downhill on FR 1706, passing a junction on the left with Forest Road 1762 at **20.8** miles. Turn right and continue on FR 1706 as it drops to join the paved road to Boulder Cave at **22.0** miles. Turn left and follow the paved road past Camp Roganunda to the Boulder Cave Picnic Area, **23.0** miles from the Clover Springs intersection.

The trail to Boulder Cave is about 0.8 mile, climbing at a moderate grade above a canyon walled by cliffs carved by Devil's Creek. The trail branches at 0.7 mile, with the right fork dropping down into the cave entrance. It's totally dark in the cave, which is several hundred yards long, and if you plan to follow the trail through the cave, carry a flashlight and a jacket, because it is cold and pitch black. At the cave exit, the trail turns and climbs back to the junction at 0.7 mile.

You can take the short way back to Highway 410. Stay right at the junction with FR 1706 and cross the Naches River on a bridge that joins Highway 410, just west of the community of Cliffdell.

62. Canteen Flats

RATING	⦿⦿⦿⦿
DISTANCE	7.5 miles
ROAD SURFACE	Graded gravel
ROAD CONDITION	Good/Poor
ROAD GRADE	Steep
PUCKER FACTOR	Sightseeing OK
ACCESSIBLE	Summer, fall
LAND MANAGER/CONTACT	Okanogan-Wenatchee National Forest, Naches Ranger District, (509) 653-1401, www.fs.usda.gov/okawen
NOTES	Rocky road improves after the first mile

The Drive

You can't beat the meadow at Canteen Flats for your own giant picnic grounds, just a short trip from a busy highway.

Getting There

Follow Highway 410 east from Cliffdell for 7.7 miles to the junction with the Bald Mountain Road, Forest Road 1701. If driving west, follow Highway 410 for 1.3 miles west of the Nile Loop Road detour. (See map on page 183.) GPS location: N46°52.250'; W120°58.156'

The Road

This drive was one of the nicest surprises I encountered while earning a fine patina of dust all over my trusty auto. It begins on a barren, hot, southeast-facing slope and climbs steeply along a bumpy, lumpy road paved with sharp rocks for about **1.0** mile. You'll look down to Highway 410 and rooftops that you might hit if you dropped a penny off the side of the road. OK—it's not that steep. But it sure looks like it.

After slowly negotiating the rocks and bumps of the road, Forest Road 1701 gets a bit tamer as it turns from the sunny south slope to the shady northwest side and climbs into a nice pine forest. The shade here is welcome, especially on the frequent summer days when the mercury hits 90 degrees or more. You'll climb in **1.7** miles to a junction with Forest Road 1711 on the right, and stay left on FR 1701.

Beyond, you'll enter the Mount Baker–Snoqualmie National Forest at **2.2** miles, although the Okanogan-Wenatchee National Forest manages this section. Here the road turns and climbs to a wide forested plateau and a junction

Canteen Flats: appropriate name.

near a stock loading area with Forest Roads 1712 and 1713, **4.0** miles from Highway 410.

Keep left at the junction and pass a junction with Forest Road 517 at mile **4.6**, where you'll stay right. The road now climbs a west-facing hillside decorated with alpine wildflowers, and it's a good idea to stop here before you ogle the spectacular view of Mount Rainier, the Tatoosh Range, and Goat Rocks Wilderness to the left, **5.3** miles from the highway.

At **5.9** miles, the road crests a forested ridge and you might be tempted to turn around here for fear of losing the view. Trust me: things will get better. The road forks here, and you'll keep right as you wind gently downhill for about 1.0 mile before keeping left at a junction with Forest Road 522. Here FR 1701 turns left and crosses Canteen Flats, a splendid spot for a picnic **7.5** miles from the highway.

Canteen Flats is well named. It's big enough to house a regulation football field and flat as a pancake griddle. Grab the blanket and picnic basket, find a viewpoint of Mount Rainier to your liking, and celebrate life.

63. McDaniel Lake

RATING ⊛⊛
DISTANCE 12.0 miles
ROAD SURFACE Paved/Graded gravel
ROAD CONDITION Good
ROAD GRADE Steep
PUCKER FACTOR Flatlanders welcome
ACCESSIBLE Summer, fall
LAND MANAGER/CONTACT Okanogan-Wenatchee National Forest, Naches Ranger District, (509) 653-1401, www.fs.usda.gov/okawen
NOTES Lake is shallow and grassy

The Drive

The nicest part about this outing is the quiet meadow and forest around the lake, where surprisingly few bugs spoil the scene.

Getting There

Drive east on Highway 410 to the Nile Loop Road, the detour around the 2009 landslide that destroyed 0.5 mile of Highway 410, and turn right to cross the Naches River on the Nile Loop Road. Follow this road for 3.3 miles to the Bethel Ridge Road, Forest Road 1500, and turn right.

If driving west, turn left at the Nile Loop Road detour at milepost 108 and follow the Nile Loop Road for 1.4 miles and turn left on the Bethel Ridge Road. GPS location: N46°49.139'; W120°56.006'

Note: The Nile Loop Road has a 35-mile-per-hour speed limit, which is rabidly enforced by friendly Washington State Patrol troopers. You have been warned.

The Road

This drive passes by some colorfully named scenery. To begin with, there's Rattlesnake Creek and Little Rattlesnake Creek, which was named not because the snakes were any smaller, but (as you probably have guessed by now) because this creek isn't as big as Rattlesnake Creek.

And there's Logger Canyon, which undoubtedly got its name because at some point, loggers worked there. Then you'll pass under Cowpuncher Ridge to the east, where I am reasonably certain very few sheepherders congregated. Finally, you'll drive past some "diverse" campsites dubbed the Hanging Tree Campground on the map. Here, scenes for the 1959 movie *The Hanging Tree*

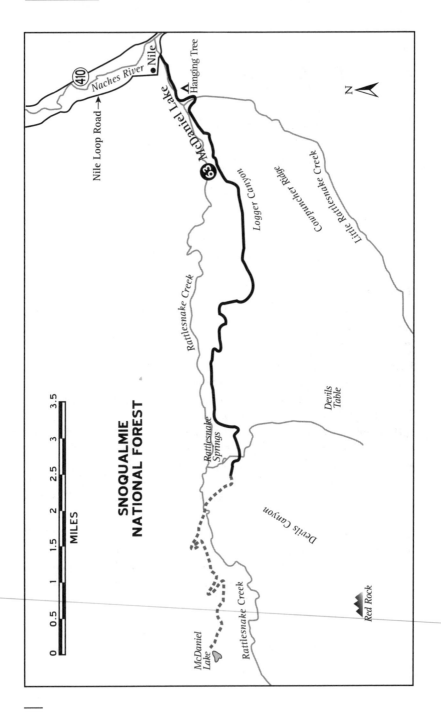

McDaniel Lake lies in a pretty meadow.

were filmed. It starred Gary Cooper, Maria Schell, Karl Malden, and George C. Scott.

First, drive to a bridge and junction with the Little Rattlesnake Road, which was closed by a big washout in the winter of 2010–2011 and is gated at the junction. Just beyond, you'll see a flat area in trees off to the left where the movie was filmed, **1.2** miles from the Nile Loop Road. A sign here indicates McDaniel Lake is 11.0 miles distant.

Now you'll begin climbing above Rattlesnake Creek along Logger Canyon and leave the Oak Creek Wildlife Area to enter the Okanogan-Wenatchee National Forest, **5.6** miles. The pavement ends at a junction with Forest Road 1500 at mile **7.9**. FR 1500 turns left here and in 18.0 miles, joins White Pass Highway 12 (drive #68). You'll turn right on Forest Road 1502, dropping down to Rattlesnake Springs Junction at **8.0** miles and crossing Rattlesnake Creek, **8.4** miles from the Nile Loop Road.

Climb high above the Rattlesnake Creek canyon to a cliffside view at **9.5** miles, then follow a bumpy FR 1502 as it passes "diverse" campsites and four-wheel-drive trails leading down to a forested swale. The road climbs again and at **11.9** miles, joins the spur leading down to McDaniel Lake. Huge pine trees shade a quiet camping spot that looks across the shallow lake and meadow beyond, and the solitude and calm forest surrounds you.

A smaller lake is about 0.2 mile farther up FR 1502, while a third pond separates the two. Forest Road 1502 continues another rough 2.0 miles beyond the lake, ending near the boundary of the William O. Douglas Wilderness to the west.

HIGHWAY 12

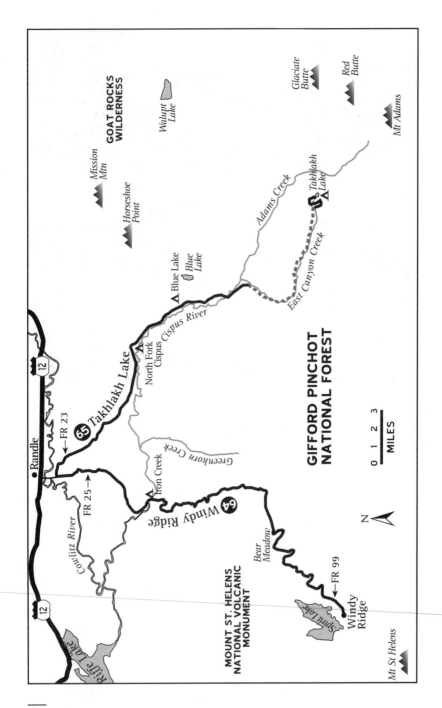

GOAT ROCKS
WILDERNESS

Glaciate
Butte

Red
Butte

Walupt
Lake

Mt Adams

Mission
Mtn

Horseshoe
Point

Takhlakh
Lake

Adams Creek

Blue Lake

Blue
Lake

East Canyon Creek

Cispus River

North Fork
Cispus

Takhlakh Lake

12

Randle

FR 23

65

GIFFORD PINCHOT
NATIONAL FOREST

0 1 2 3
MILES

Greenhorn Creek

Iron Creek

FR 25

Cowlitz River

64 Windy Ridge

N

Bear
Meadow

FR 99

MOUNT ST. HELENS
NATIONAL VOLCANIC
MONUMENT

12

Spirit Lake

Windy
Ridge

Mt St Helens

Riffe Lake

64. Windy Ridge

RATING	✿✿✿✿
DISTANCE	36.1 miles
ROAD SURFACE	Paved
ROAD CONDITION	Good
ROAD GRADE	Steep
PUCKER FACTOR	Sightseeing OK
ACCESSIBLE	Summer, fall
LAND MANAGER/CONTACT	Mount St. Helens National Volcanic Monument, (360) 449-7800, www.fs.usda.gov/mountsthelens
TRAILHEADS	Norway Pass, Harmony Falls
CAMPGROUNDS	Iron Creek
NOTES	Northwest Forest Pass ($5 daily, $30 annually) required

The Drive

If you haven't driven up to the Windy Ridge Interpretive Center at the Mount St. Helens National Volcanic Monument, you've got to do it now. If you have done it, do it again.

Getting There

Take Highway 12 to Randle and turn right on Highway 131, the Cowlitz River bridge. GPS location: N46°32.112'; W121°57.425'

The Road

Windy Ridge is one of the best places to see what happened on May 18, 1980, when Mount St. Helens blew its top. You can look down into the crater, which was once part of the mountain rising from where you stand, to the summit of the peak, more than 1,000 feet above where it is today. It is an impressive place to be, where you've a graphic demonstration of the power of nature.

Cross the Cowlitz River and follow Highway 131—County Road 9009—passing the junction with Forest Road 23 (drive #65) at **1.1** miles. Keep right and follow Woods Creek Road for 5.6 miles past the Woods Creek Information Center to the junction of Woods Creek Road and Forest Road 25 and turn left, **7.4** miles.

From the junction, FR 25 turns south, passing a junction with Forest Road 26 at **8.7** miles, where you'll turn left on FR 25. Cross the Cispus River and

A climb from the parking area at Windy Ridge leads to a great view of Mount St. Helens.

pass Iron Creek Campground at **9.7** miles, then follow FR 25 to the right just past the campground. You'll begin climbing in the forest, crossing Benham and Fourmile Creeks before reaching a junction with Forest Road 99, **19.6** miles from Randle.

Turn right onto Forest Road 99 and pass the Wakepish Sno-Park, which in the summer is a drop-off point for trailers that are not permitted on the steep, narrow road above. FR 99 climbs in forest into the alpine country around the Bear Meadow Viewpoint, **24.0** miles. Continue another 3.7 miles to a junction with Forest Road 26, which turns north to the Norway Pass trailhead. You'll continue to the left and pass the Miners' Car Interpretive Center and at **33.1** miles, arrive at the Harmony Falls Viewpoint. A trail leads down to Spirit Lake at the viewpoint. Smith Creek Viewpoint is another 2.0 miles along the ridge and Windy Ridge is another 1.0 mile beyond.

65. Takhlakh Lake

RATING	⊛⊛⊛⊛⊛
DISTANCE	32.3 miles
ROAD SURFACE	Paved/Graded gravel
ROAD CONDITION	Good
ROAD GRADE	Moderate
PUCKER FACTOR	Flatlanders welcome
ACCESSIBLE	Summer, fall
LAND MANAGER/CONTACT	Gifford Pinchot National Forest, Mount Adams Ranger District, (509) 395-3400, www.fs.fed.us/gpnf
TRAILHEADS	Blue Lake
CAMPGROUNDS	North Fork Cispus, Blue Lake, Takhlakh Lake
NOTES	Northwest Forest Pass ($5 daily, $30 annually) required

The Drive

Here's one of the best Sunday drives in the state. It follows tumbling rivers through evergreen forests, then climbs to a high lake with the best view of Mount Adams to be found anywhere.

Getting There

Take Highway 12 to Randle and turn right on Highway 131, the Cowlitz River bridge. (See map on page 196.) GPS location: N46°32.112'; W121°57.425'

The Road

Takhlakh Lake and its campground are extremely popular in the summer, and with good reason. The campground serves up some of the nicest tent camping to be found anywhere in the state and there's a separate loop for RVs. You can picnic above the lake and look across at the Adams Glacier, frozen in mid-fall from the summit of 12,281-foot Mount Adams, second-highest peak in Washington.

You can walk around the lake on an easy trail and visit nearby lava flows. Neighboring lakes in alpine meadows offer their own beauty, and you're east of the Cascade crest, so expect some sunshine. If there's a single problem with this drive, it's that the lake is 4,385 feet above sea level, which means Old Man Winter refuses to leave at a respectable hour. In 2011, for example, some of the campsites at Takhlakh were covered by the white stuff in early August.

Takhlakh Lake and Mount Adams.

The campground is usually open until the last weekend of September and the general area is crowded with hunters. Late fall is a good time to visit, but you'll probably have to walk down the road for about 0.25 mile to the campground and picnic sites.

Begin by crossing the Cowlitz River and driving **1.0** mile on Highway 131 to its junction with Forest Road 23 and turn left. FR 23 is paved almost the entire way to the lake, and makes an excellent route to the Columbia River Gorge if you're in no hurry and want to see some scenery. At **3.5** miles, keep left at a junction with Forest Road 2504, where you'll cross Squire Creek.

Beyond, FR 23 continues south, passing Forest Roads 2305 and 2306 at **4.7** miles from Randle. Next, at **5.1** miles, stay right and pass Forest Road 55, then stay left where Forest Road 2308 joins FR 23, **7.3** miles. You'll pass a junction with Forest Road 28, **8.0** miles, and soon be driving up the Cispus River valley under a forest canopy of old evergreens and alder. Stay right at a junction with Forest Road 22 and pass the two North Fork Cispus campgrounds, **10.6** miles.

The road climbs a forested hillside above the river, **12.5** miles from Randle, before dropping back to the riverside and following the river close to its banks for about 1.0 mile. Then the road climbs past the Blue Lake Campground and trailhead, **15.2** miles, before arriving at a junction with Forest Road 21, **17.6** miles from Randle.

Turn right and continue on FR 23 as it crosses the Cispus River at **18.4** miles, and begin climbing in forest above East Canyon Creek, where the road turns to gravel. The grade becomes steeper as you wind above the creek and at about **25.0** miles, reach flat meadows ringed by forest, where you get a hint of the spectacular views ahead. At **30.5** miles, arrive at a junction with Forest Road 2329, and turn left onto FR 2329, which is paved.

Drive about 2.0 miles up FR 2329, passing Forest Road 5601 to Olallie Lake, then turn right at **32.0** miles to the Takhlakh Lake Campground. The best views of Mount Adams are from the walk-in tent campsites to the left.

If you want to drive farther, or are taking the scenic route to the Columbia Gorge, return to FR 23 and turn left. This is the worst of the gravel road and leads in 2.0 miles to a spectacular view of Mount Adams as you drop into the Lewis River valley. FR 23 turns to pavement in a few more miles and heads south through forestland for about 24.0 miles to Trout Lake. To reach the Columbia Gorge, follow Highway 141 to White Salmon.

66. South Fork Tieton River

RATING	⚙⚙
DISTANCE	12.6 miles
ROAD SURFACE	Paved/Graded gravel
ROAD CONDITION	Fair
ROAD GRADE	Moderate
PUCKER FACTOR	Flatlanders welcome
ACCESSIBLE	Summer, fall
LAND MANAGER/CONTACT	Okanogan-Wenatchee National Forest, Naches Ranger District, (509) 653-1401, www.fs.usda.gov/okawen
CAMPGROUNDS	South Fork Group, Grey Creek
NOTES	Northwest Forest Pass ($5 daily, $30 annually) required

The Drive

The road to Minnie Meadows provides nice scenery along the canyon of the South Fork of the Tieton River, ending at a great picnic area and "diverse" camping.

Getting There

From the west, follow Highway 410 to Cayuse Pass and Highway 123 to its junction with Highway 12, then take Highway 12 for 29 miles east over White Pass to the junction with the Tieton Road, Forest Road 1200. If driving from the east, follow Highway 12 for 19 miles west of Naches to the Tieton Road. GPS location: N46°40.281'; W121°05.206'

The Road

From the miles before you reach Minnie Meadows, a long, green field along the South Fork of the Tieton River, you might not imagine getting so close to the river without climbing down a steep cliff. Take courage: the road eventually leads to riverside picnicking and "diverse" campsites.

Begin by following the Tieton Road, Forest Road 1200, as it crosses the Tieton River and climbs into a canyon formed by Chimney Rocks to the south and Goose Egg Mountain to the north. The Tieton Road (drive #67) circles Rimrock and Clearwater Lakes back to Highway 12. After **3.6** miles, the road drops back down to Rimrock Lake and reaches a junction with the Fish Creek Road, Forest Road 1203, at **4.1** miles. Just beyond, cross the outlet

The South Fork of the Tieton River rambles through big pine forests.

of the South Fork Tieton River and at **4.6** miles, turn left on the South Fork Tieton Road, Forest Road 1000.

You'll pass the South Fork Group Campground on the left in a splendid old ponderosa pine forest before you reach Jayhawk Flats, a popular "diverse" camping area along the lower South Fork, **5.8** miles from Highway 12. Beyond, the road climbs above the river as it rolls through a steep-walled canyon.

In about 4.0 miles, it passes Bakeoven Flats, which as you can probably guess, gets pretty darn hot in the summer. The pavement ends at Grey Creek, **10.4** miles from the highway. You'll reach a junction with Forest Road 1040 at **11.6** miles and keep left, arriving at the north end of Minnie Meadows at **12.6** miles.

Spread the blanket out. Settle in. Enjoy the scenery.

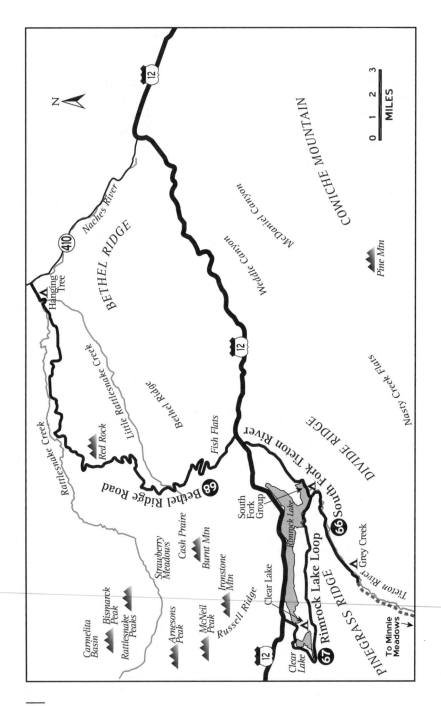

67. Rimrock Lake Loop

RATING	⦿⦿⦿
DISTANCE	16.6 miles
ROAD SURFACE	Paved
ROAD CONDITION	Excellent
ROAD GRADE	Moderate
PUCKER FACTOR	Flatlanders welcome
ACCESSIBLE	Year-round
LAND MANAGER/CONTACT	Wenatchee National Forest, Naches Ranger District, (509) 653-1401, www.fs.usda.gov/okawen
CAMPGROUNDS	Clear Lake (2)
NOTES	Northwest Forest Pass ($5 daily, $30 annually) required at picnic areas; Washington State Sno-Park permit ($20–$40 annually) required at Sno-Park areas in winter

The Drive

Here's a scenic loop trip around two pretty lakes high in the southern Cascades, providing year-round recreation.

Getting There

From the west, follow Highway 410 to Cayuse Pass and Highway 123 to its junction with Highway 12, then take Highway 12 for 29 miles east over White Pass to the junction with the Tieton Road, Forest Road 1200. If driving from the east, follow Highway 12 for 19 miles west of Naches to the Tieton Road. (See map on page 206.) GPS location: N46°40.281'; W121°05.206'

The Road

This drive is a popular getaway both in summer and winter. In summer, use it to escape from the relatively more crowded side of Rimrock and Clear Lakes along the Highway 12 corridor. It's generally quieter along the southern side of Rimrock. The Tieton River is crawling—or rather, splashing—with white-water kayakers and raft riders every September, when water from Rimrock Lake is released.

And in winter, the Tieton loop is a nice drive for those searching for their own spot to play in the snow or go snowmobiling, snowshoeing, or cross-country skiing. A number of Sno-Park areas are located off the road,

Drive around Clear Lake on the Rimrock Lake Loop.

including a popular snowmobile Sno-Park on the east end of Rimrock Lake and a nonmotorized Sno-Park on the west end of Clear Lake.

Begin by following the paved road as it climbs in pine forest between dark chocolate basalt cliffs on either side of the road, passing the Ghormley Meadow Road **0.2** mile from the highway. Stay right and at **1.5** miles, pass the Milk Creek Road with its view of Chimney Rocks. Stay on the main road and in another 1.0 mile, Rimrock Lake comes into view and you'll pass a road on the left leading to the Rimrock recreation area and landing strip, a popular snowmobiling spot in the winter.

The road drops to lake level, passing the Fish Creek Road on the left about **4.0** miles from the highway. The road rounds a corner at lake level and at **4.3** miles, joins with the South Fork Tieton Road (drive #66). Stay right for the lake loop as the road climbs away from the water into pine forest, with views down to the water and access roads dropping to "diverse" campsites along the lake.

Stay right at **11.1** miles, passing Forest Road 1205 and shortly after, pass Forest Road 12740 on the left. This road leads to campgrounds and picnic areas on Clear Lake. This smaller lake above Rimrock is a quiet alternative, populated more often in the summer by campers and anglers. The view to the west from the boat launch at the east end of the lake includes snow-hoarding Cascade peaks around White Pass and the Goat Rocks Wilderness.

Next, you'll find the North Fork Tieton Road, Forest Road 1207, on the left. This 5.0-mile gravel road provides access to trails that climb into the Goat Rocks Wilderness and join the Pacific Crest Trail, which stretches from Mexico to Canada. If you're looking for a quiet picnic spot, it makes a good side trip to the parking area at the end of the road, where you'll find a whispering stream at the trailhead. The road is closed in the winter and a non-motorized Sno-Park makes a good snowshoeing or cross-country ski outing.

Beyond the junction, the road rounds the end of Clear Lake, passing a private group camp and several residences before rejoining Highway 12, just west of Indian Creek Campground. It's about 9.0 miles west to the White Pass summit.

68. Bethel Ridge Road

RATING	✪✪✪
DISTANCE	25.4 miles
ROAD SURFACE	Graded gravel/Paved
ROAD CONDITION	Good
ROAD GRADE	Steep
PUCKER FACTOR	Sightseeing OK
ACCESSIBLE	Summer, fall
LAND MANAGER/CONTACT	Okanogan-Wenatchee National Forest, Naches Ranger District, (509) 653-1401, www.fs.usda.gov/okawen
NOTES	Hot and dusty in summer

The Drive

Use this road to take the relaxed, scenic route from the White Pass Highway to the Chinook Pass Highway.

Getting There

Drive 3 miles east from the Highway 12 tunnel at Rimrock Lake to the junction with Forest Road 1500 and turn left. (See map on page 206.) GPS location: N46°40.534'; W121°04.807'

The Road

If you've ever driven the scenic highway loop that crosses White Pass on Highway 12, then returns via Chinook Pass on Highway 410, you might want to try this variation that climbs over a pass on beautiful Bethel Ridge that is about 1,000 feet higher than either White or Chinook Passes. The saddle at Bethel Ridge is a great place to stop and admire the view, and is roughly halfway between the two highways.

Forest Road 1500 over Bethel Ridge starts with a steep climb in numerous switchbacks through open forest. Because it faces south, it's good to begin this climb early in the morning when it might be cooler. In **0.5** mile, you'll pass two road spurs on the right before arriving at a junction with Forest Road 1304, **1.5** miles from the highway. Stay left and continue climbing in steep hairpin corners at **2.2** miles and **4.3** miles.

The road continues to climb relentlessly, reaching a junction with Forest Road 390 at **5.1** miles. Follow FR 1500 to the left and climb into an open slope with great views to the south before switching back again near a junction

The Bethel Ridge Road begins in tall pines and climbs to sweeping mountain views.

with Forest Road 324 at **6.5** miles. You've climbed about 3,000 vertical feet, but you're not finished.

FR 1500 turns left and climbs past Forest Road 199 at **6.7** miles, finally reaching the Bethel Ridge, 5,709 feet above sea level. Mountains in every direction. Forests and rocky canyons below. Take it all in before dropping down into the Little Rattlesnake canyon, where the road drops steeply and passes several spur roads before arriving at a junction with Forest Road 1506, **11.7** miles from Highway 12. Turn right on FR 1500 here.

The road continues to wind down the Little Rattlesnake canyon, passing spur roads at **13.3** and **14.9** miles before joining Forest Road 1504 at **16.5** miles. Turn right on FR 1500 and drive a short 0.5 mile to a junction with Forest Road 1503, and follow FR 1500 to the left here. At mile **17.5**, you'll reach a junction with Forest Road 1502, which heads west to McDaniel Lake (drive #63). Turn right on the paved road and in 2.0 miles, enter the Oak Creek Wildlife Area along Logger Canyon.

You'll drop down the Rattlesnake Creek canyon, reaching a bridge and one of the sites where the movie *The Hanging Tree* was filmed in the late 1950s, **24.2** miles from Highway 12. From there, the Bethel Ridge Road arrives at a junction with the Nile Loop Road, the detour around the massive landslide on Highway 410. Westbound traffic should turn left on the Nile Loop Road and join Highway 410 in 3.3 miles. Traffic head to Naches and Yakima can turn right, joining Highway 410 in 1.4 miles. Washington State Patrol troopers regularly catch speeders on the Nile Loop Road, so make certain you adhere to the 35-mile-per-hour limit.

69. Oak Creek Wildlife Area

RATING	❸❸❸
DISTANCE	5.8 miles
ROAD SURFACE	Graded gravel
ROAD CONDITION	Fair
ROAD GRADE	Moderate
PUCKER FACTOR	Flatlanders welcome
ACCESSIBLE	Summer, fall
LAND MANAGER/CONTACT	Oak Creek Wildlife Area, (509) 653-2390, www.wdfw.wa.gov/lands/wildlife_areas/oak_creek
NOTES	Discover Pass ($10 daily, $30–$35 annually) required

The Drive

Here's a sunny drive up a barren canyon filled with wildlife-watching opportunities.

Getting There

From the Highway 410–Highway 12 junction, 4 miles west of Naches, turn south on Highway 12 and drive 2 miles to the Oak Creek Wildlife Area headquarters, on the right. Continue past the headquarters on Highway 12 to the junction with the Oak Creek Road and turn right. GPS location: N46°43.434'; W120°48.862'

The Road

It's what's at the beginning of this road that makes the drive interesting, because it is one of the few places where you can get within 10 feet of a real, live, wild bull elk. You can barely get this close to these magnificent animals in a zoo, and the elk at the Oak Creek Wildlife Area are anything but zoo animals.

The program began seven decades ago, when the state Department of Natural Resources and the Department of Fish and Wildlife began acquiring land around Oak Creek to give a growing herd of elk someplace other than orchards for them to winter. Elk migrate from their summer homes high in the central Cascades to the 47,200-acre wildlife area, where they are fed during the winter months and where volunteers can explain the program and feed the elk.

The Oak Creek Road, Forest Road 1400, is closed in March and April to protect herds of elk and other wildlife that call the area home. Besides the big

Basalt columns across from the Oak Creek Wildlife Area.

buglers, you might see mule deer and bighorn sheep, which are fed at several stations where you'll need to display your Discover Pass. Other wildlife in the area include forest grouse, turkey, quail, wood duck, and a bunch of reptiles and amphibians (including rattlesnakes!).

The best time to go, unless you intend to visit the winter feeding program and skip the drive, would be in early May, when the barren hills above Oak Creek might still have some green in them. It gets mighty hot in the summer, and the Oregon white oak that give the creek its name just don't provide that much shade.

The road climbs north above the Oak Creek canyon, which is lined with scrub cottonwood and access is limited. Keep a lookout along the stream for bald and even golden eagles scouting for a meal. Look for deer along the edges of the creek and bighorn sheep on slopes above.

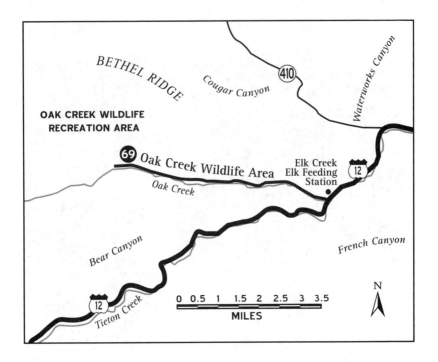

The road winds more than 10.0 miles up the creek canyon and connects with myriad roads that climb into the high steppes and grasslands, but you'll probably see everything you want by the time you reach the north fork of Oak Creek, **5.8** miles from the highway. Continue on, if you've not seen any wildlife by then.

MOUNT RAINIER

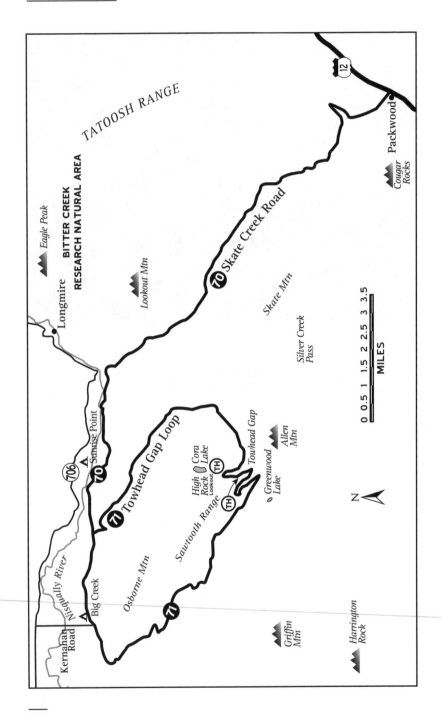

70. Skate Creek Road

RATING	✪✪✪
DISTANCE	23.0 miles
ROAD SURFACE	Paved
ROAD CONDITION	Good
ROAD GRADE	Moderate
PUCKER FACTOR	Flatlanders welcome
ACCESSIBLE	Spring–fall
LAND MANAGER/CONTACT	Gifford Pinchot National Forest, (360) 497-1100, www.fs.fed.us/gpnf
CAMPGROUNDS	Big Creek
NOTES	Great weekend drive

The Drive

The Skate Creek Road provides summer and fall access from Highway 706 to Ashford and from Mount Rainier National Park to the White Pass Highway 12.

Getting There

From Ashford, follow Highway 706 east for about 2 miles to the Kernahan Road and turn right. GPS location: N46°45.431'; W121°58.874'

The Road

Most motorists heading to the White Pass Highway follow Highway 7 from Elbe to Morton, which is a nice road if you're interested in getting there at highway speeds and driving past clear-cuts and "urban" areas like Morton and Packwood. If you'd prefer a kinder, gentler pace with the opportunity to spot wildlife and get a great view of Mount Rainier, try the Skate Creek Road. It's a favorite of the laid-back community around Ashford and others who aren't in a hurry to get anywhere.

Begin by following the Kernahan Road south past private homes and crossing the Nisqually River to the Skate Creek Road, Forest Road 52, **1.4** miles from Highway 706. Turn left and pass the Big Creek Campground in another 0.5 mile. You'll be following the Nisqually River upstream where you'll get a view of Mount Rainier above the trees. At **4.8** miles, pass Forest Road 8440 (drive #71), which climbs to Towhead Gap.

Beyond, the road continues to climb, passing a gate where, as snows of winter deepen, the road is closed. The mountain rises above the forest again at around **5.7** miles, near the entrance to Mount Rainier National Park, across

Sunshine Point Campground is just across the Nisqually River from Skate Creek Road.

the Nisqually River. You'll be driving south and at **9.2** miles, arrive at a low pass and junction with a road leading up Horse Creek. Turn right here and pass big Bear Meadows on the right, a good place to scan for wildlife.

You've crossed over into the Skate Creek drainage and you're driving down the Skate Creek canyon, surrounded by a lowland forest of alder, fir, and cedar. Find a number of dispersed campsites along the road and by the river below. At **17.2** miles, cross Skate Creek where it joins with Johnson Creek and continue to a junction with the Dixon Creek Road, **18.6** miles from Highway 706. Keep left here and leave the creek valley to climb over a low hill, switchback, and drop into the Cowlitz River valley on the eastern outskirts of Packwood. Cross the Cowlitz River at **22.5** miles and join White Pass Highway 12, **23.0** miles from Highway 26.

For a longer ride, turn east on Highway 12 to Randle, then follow Forest Road 25 to Mount St. Helens National Volcanic Monument (drive #64). Another option: take Forest Road 23 from Randle to Takhlakh Lake (drive #65).

71. Towhead Gap Loop

RATING	⊕⊕⊕⊕⊕
DISTANCE	26.3 miles
ROAD SURFACE	Paved/Graded gravel
ROAD CONDITION	Good
ROAD GRADE	Steep
PUCKER FACTOR	Sightseeing OK
ACCESSIBLE	Summer, fall
LAND MANAGER/CONTACT	Gifford Pinchot National Forest, Cowlitz Ranger District, (360) 497-1100, www.fs.fed.us/gpnf
TRAILHEADS	Cora Lake, High Rock Lookout
CAMPGROUNDS	Big Creek
NOTES	Northwest Forest Pass ($5 daily, $30 annually) required to park at Towhead Gap

The Drive

This forest road leads to one of the best views of Mount Rainier outside the national park, and to a steep, short hike to an even more spectacular view at the old High Rock fire lookout.

Getting There

From Ashford, follow Highway 706 east for about 2 miles to the Kernahan Road and turn right. (See map on page 216.) GPS location: N46°45.431'; W121°58.874'

The Road

Beginning near the Nisqually entrance to Mount Rainier National Park, this drive takes you from river level to almost a mile high. The scenery changes from a typical wet Northwest forest to lofty views of the Nisqually River valley below to a stunning vista of 14,411-foot-high Mount Rainier. Day-hikers head up this road to walk the steep 1.6-mile trail to High Rock Lookout, which you can see from the road, perched at the prow of a massive cliff face to the north.

From the intersection of Highway 706 with the Kernahan Road, follow the Kernahan Road as it passes a number of private residences and crosses the Nisqually River, less than 20.0 miles from where the river is born at the toe of the Nisqually Glacier in the park. At **1.5** miles, you'll arrive at the intersection with the Skate Creek Road, Forest Road 52. Turn left and follow the Skate Creek Road to its junction with Forest Road 8440, **4.8** miles from the highway.

High Rock Lookout is about a mile from Towhead Gap.

Turn right onto FR 8440, where the pavement ends. The road may be washboarded at its beginning, but improves as it climbs out of the lowland forest. You'll round a curve to the south at **6.3** miles and cross Mesatchee Creek **6.9** miles from the highway. A number of forest roads branch off FR 8440, but they are easily distinguished from the main road. One such road leads to the right and a rock quarry **7.9** miles from the highway.

You'll cross Big Creek at mile **8.3** and arrive at a junction with a forest road **11.6** miles from the highway. Keep right here and begin a steady climb to a sweeping switchback at **13.2** miles, where the first of two trails leads north to Cora Lake. You can look above the forest canopy as you round this curve to the 600-foot sheer cliff of the High Rock and its lookout. The final climb to Towhead Gap is to the south, where your side-view mirror will be dominated by Mount Rainier.

The trail to High Rock Lookout climbs about 1,400 vertical feet in 1.6 miles, following the ridge north from Towhead Gap. If you'd like a strenuous hike leading to a spectacular and airy view of Rainier, this is it. Most motorists, however, are content with the view at Towhead Gap.

To close the loop, continue around the hairpin corner at Towhead Gap and switchback downhill on Forest Road 8440 for 4.5 miles to a junction with Forest Road 85, then bear right onto FR 85 and drive 6.0 miles to its junction with the Kernahan Road. Turn left and follow the Kernahan Road back to Highway 706.

72. Mowich Lake

RATING	⦿⦿⦿⦿⦿
DISTANCE	16.5 miles
ROAD SURFACE	Graded gravel
ROAD CONDITION	Fair/Poor
ROAD GRADE	Steep
PUCKER FACTOR	Flatlanders welcome
ACCESSIBLE	Summer, fall
LAND MANAGER/CONTACT	Mount Rainier National Park, Carbon River Ranger Station, (360) 829-9639, www.nps.gov/mora
TRAILHEADS	Paul Peak, Spray Park, Eunice Lake, Ipsut Pass
CAMPGROUNDS	Mowich Lake
NOTES	$15 per carload self-pay entry fee at Paul Peak trailhead

The Drive

Here's a beautiful drive to an alpine lake where the view of Mount Rainier is best from the road.

Getting There

Follow Highway 410 south from Enumclaw to Buckley and turn south on Highway 165. Follow Highway 165 through Wilkeson and Carbonado to the junction with the Carbon River Road and turn right on Highway 165. GPS location: N47°02.000'; W122°02.362'

The Road

The Mowich Lake Road is a favorite with die-hard skiers and snowboarders who hike from the end of the road into the alpine country and year-round snowfields and glaciers above Spray Park. Tent campers enjoy the lake's walk-in campground, and families with young children take the short hike to Eunice Lake or the Tolmie Peak Lookout. It's an excellent choice for a fall picnic, after the bugs of summer are gone.

The road climbs away from the Carbon River in an alder forest at a gentle pace, reaching a broad ridge in about 2.0 miles, where clear-cuts and logged private lands provide the views across ridges and valleys to the west and Mount Rainier to the south. You'll wind past a number of road junctions as you climb, but the gravel Highway 165 is easily followed. It's one of only a

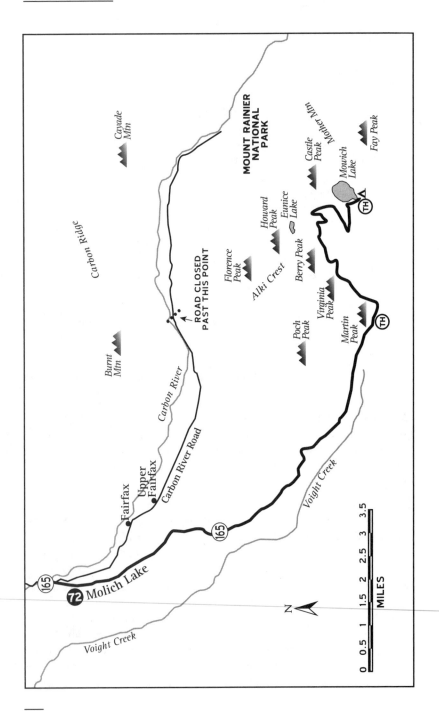

A trail winds along the northwest side of Mowich Lake.

few state highways that isn't paved. Spur roads off the highway are popular with ATV and dirt bike riders.

The view of Mount Rainier from the upper reaches of the road is spectacular, with the Carbon and Puyallup glaciers and Liberty Ridge rising to the summit. You can see the broad snowfields of the remnant Flett Glacier as well as Observation Rock.

You'll arrive at the Mount Rainier National Park boundary at **10.9** miles, and continue to the Paul Peak trailhead, **11.6** miles from the Carbon River Road. A self-pay fee station is located here, where you can pay the $15 per carload entrance fee. Pass a gate beyond the trailhead, where the road is closed in the winter and spring and where the surface deteriorates into a maze of large potholes.

Paul Peak and the Elizabeth Ridge hide Mount Rainier from view as you drive above alpine meadows and forest, switching back under Tolmie Peak at **14.5** miles. On your return trip, remember to look up at this spot to see the Tolmie Peak Lookout. The road climbs another 1.0 mile, treating you to views to the northwest before switching back and making the final steep climb to round a forested ridge at Mowich Lake, **16.2** miles. The road is usually lined with parked autos in the summer and there's a small parking area near the road's end at **16.5** miles. The campground is located across the outlet stream, where the trail to Spray Park begins.

A lakefront trail starts near the campground and follows the south and west shore of Mowich Lake for about 0.6 mile before climbing steeply for 0.5 mile to Ipsut Pass, where it branches to Eunice Lake and Ipsut Creek Campground.

EASTERN WASHINGTON

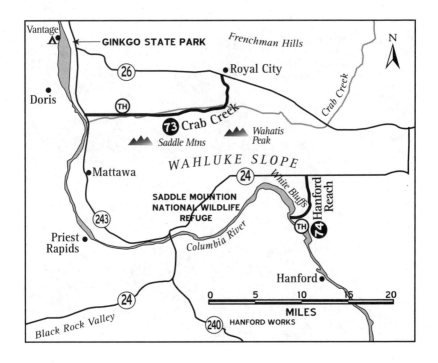

73. Crab Creek

RATING	⊛⊛⊛⊛
DISTANCE	19.8 miles
ROAD SURFACE	Graded gravel
ROAD CONDITION	Good
ROAD GRADE	Flat
PUCKER FACTOR	Flatlanders welcome
ACCESSIBLE	Year-round
LAND MANAGER/CONTACT	Washington Department of Fish and Wildlife, (509) 575-2740, www.wdfw.wa.gov
TRAILHEADS	Crab Creek
NOTES	Discover Pass ($10 daily, $30–$35 annually) required

The Drive

Here's a sunny drive through unusual and scenic landscape, along what has been called the "longest creek in the United States."

Getting There

From I-90 at Vantage, cross the Columbia River and take exit 137, turning south on Highway 26. Drive a short mile to Highway 243 and turn right. Follow Highway 243 for 7.4 miles to the Lower Crab Creek Road and turn left. GPS location: N46°49.977'; W119°56.198'

The Road

One of the nicest things about driving an Eastern Washington thoroughfare like the Crab Creek Road is that wildlife-spotting is made easy because there are no pesky trees to get in the way. The downside? It gets mighty hot here in the summer, and unless you bring your own, shade is a rare commodity.

Surrounded by the Columbia National Wildlife Refuge, the Crab Creek Coulee is a prime spot for watching winged residents like great blue herons, geese, and red-winged and yellow-headed blackbirds. Coyotes and rabbits trot and hop across the road, which follows the lower Crab Creek along the abandoned Chicago–St. Paul–Milwaukee Railroad grade.

Crab Creek stretches for 163.0 miles upstream from its confluence with the Columbia River at the community of Beverly, just north of the Crab Creek Road–Highway 243 junction. Wikipedia reports it is described as the "longest ephemeral stream in North America." You can relax—you don't have to drive the entire distance to enjoy all that the area has to offer.

Crab Creek flows past the Columbia National Wildlife Refuge.

Instead, head east as the Lower Crab Creek Road climbs past the community of Beverly and at **2.2** miles, passes the Beverly Dunes on the right and enters the state-managed Crab Creek Wildlife Area. The gravel road levels off above Crab Creek, on the left, and parallels the abandoned railroad grade for about 3.0 miles before crossing the main channel of the creek, **5.7** miles from Beverly. The steep hillside of Saddle Mountain rises above the road to the east, while the creek and ponds trail alongside the road to the west below the cliffs of the Columbia National Wildlife Refuge.

At **9.0** miles from Beverly, you'll see a wide parking area on the right and a four-wheel-drive track leading toward the creek to the left. This is a good spot to walk into the broad fields toward the old railroad trestles along the creek, or to look toward the cliffs under Saddle Mountain, where you might be able to spot an ice cave in the rocks.

The road continues for 4.7 miles past the old community of Smyrna and at **15.9** miles, turns left and recrosses Crab Creek to follow the old railroad grade and climb into the narrow Red Rock Coulee. You'll wind about 4.0 miles up the Coulee and at **19.8** miles, arrive at a junction with Highway 26. You can turn left here, and follow Highway 26 through Royal City for 18.5 miles to the Highway 26-243 junction, just south of the I-90 bridge at Vantage. A more pleasant option, if you've time and inclination, is to return the way you came.

74. Hanford Reach

RATING	❋❋❋
DISTANCE	5.7 miles
ROAD SURFACE	Graded gravel
ROAD CONDITION	Fair
ROAD GRADE	Moderate
PUCKER FACTOR	Flatlanders welcome
ACCESSIBLE	Year-round
TRAILHEADS	White Bluffs
LAND MANAGER/CONTACT	Washington Department of Fish and Wildlife, (509) 575-2740, www.wdfw.wa.gov
NOTES	Discover Pass ($10 daily, $30–$35 annually) required

The Drive

Visit the last free-flowing stretch of the Columbia River as it rolls through the desert sun.

Getting There

From I-90 at Vantage, cross the Columbia River and take exit 137 to Highway 26 and turn south. Drive a short mile to Highway 243 and turn right. Follow Highway 243 for 14.2 miles to the Highway 24 Cutoff Road, 24SW, and follow it 13.9 miles to Highway 24. Turn left on Highway 24 and follow it for 9.6 miles to the entrance to the Wahluke National Wildlife Refuge on the right. Turn right, passing through a solar-powered gate. (See map on page 226.) GPS location: N46°44.294'; W119°25.558'

The Road

You'll be driving through sage desert, some of the most arid land in all of Washington, yet find one of the mightiest rivers in the nation flowing through it. The Columbia River runs free along the Hanford Reach, largely because the federal government's Hanford Nuclear Reservation is a next-door neighbor. It's the last part of the Columbia without a dam, and the boat launch at the end of the road is popular with anglers, especially in the fall when salmon and steelhead are heading upstream.

The road is straight as a compass bearing to the south and flat as a pancake griddle once past the solar gate, which closes in the evening and reopens just before dawn. You'll be traveling through sagebrush-covered plains, the unlikely home of mule deer and Rocky Mountain elk, as well as reptiles like

The last free-flowing stretch of the Columbia River runs through Hanford Reach.

rattlesnakes and lizards, which in turn support populations of raptors like red-tailed hawks. Hundreds of Canada geese and tundra swans rest here during their migration.

The road heads south for **3.9** miles to a three-way junction where you'll turn right on a road that is partially paved in broken chunks of concrete. It heads downhill to the west, curving along a barren canyon and at **5.2** miles, passes a wide parking area on the right. This is the parking area for the White Bluffs Trail, which climbs the low hill to the north and provides an excellent view of the river below. Hikers can follow the trail for as many as 4.0 miles, one-way—but the view doesn't get much better than it is in the first 1.0 mile.

Beyond the parking area, you can continue for another 0.5 mile to the boat launch, which is a good spot to settle down and watch the big old river roll past. Except for some power lines and the crowd of boat trailers and anglers, it pretty much looks the same as when Lewis and Clark passed this way, more than 200 years ago.

75. Turnbull National Wildlife Refuge

RATING	✪✪✪✪
DISTANCE	5.9-mile loop
ROAD SURFACE	Graded gravel
ROAD CONDITION	Good
ROAD GRADE	Flat
PUCKER FACTOR	Flatlanders welcome
ACCESSIBLE	Year-round
LAND MANAGER/CONTACT	Turnbull National Wildlife Refuge, (509) 235-4723, www.fws.gov/turnbull
TRAILHEADS	Kepple Lake, Kepple Lake Interpretive, Pine Lake Loop, Boardwalk, Columbia Plateau
NOTES	$3 day-use fee

The Drive

You want to see a moose? An elk? A gaggle of geese? A herd of swans? This is the place to go.

Getting There

From Highway 904 in Cheney, turn east on the South Cheney–Plaza Road and drive 4.3 miles to the Turnbull National Wildlife Refuge entrance. Turn left and drive 1.9 miles to the refuge headquarters at South Smith Road. GPS location: N47°24.939'; W117°32.040'

The Road

The Turnbull National Wildlife Refuge is one of the best places in the state to watch wildlife, and the short auto tour shouldn't be missed by anyone passing through the Spokane area. It's 16,000 acres of basalt outcrops and canyons, open ponderosa pine forests, sagebrush, and ponds that host deer, moose, elk, swans, geese, and more than 200 bird species. Coyotes, badgers, porcupine, muskrats, beaver, and river otter live here and a dozen species of bats have been seen. Best time for spotting the big animals is in the early morning or at dusk.

The auto tour route is open year-round, and you can expect to find snow in the winter. It begins at the refuge headquarters, where you'll find restrooms and a gift shop. An accessible trail is across from the headquarters at Pine Lake, and loops around the lake.

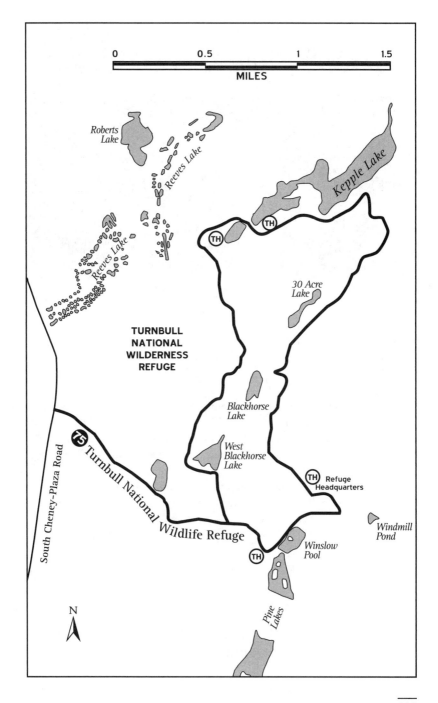

Kepple Lake, along the Turnbull National Wildlife Refuge auto tour, serves up a great view.

The auto tour begins by heading north on the Smith Road and passing Black Horse Lake at **0.9** mile, where a boardwalk trail provides viewing opportunities. Next, you'll pass 30-Acre Lake, **1.3** miles.

A second accessible trail is located at Kepple Lake, **2.3** miles from the refuge headquarters, where you'll also find a pedestrian trail leading to an overlook. Kepple is one of the likely spots for seeing waterfowl and perhaps moose.

Turn left at Kepple and follow the Pine Grove Road south across an isthmus at the end of Kepple Lake, **3.0** miles, and pass West Black Horse Lake at **4.8** miles. You'll rejoin the refuge entrance road at **5.2** miles, 0.7 mile west of the refuge headquarters.

In addition to the auto tour, several trails radiate from the headquarters for those looking for a short hike. Another opportunity to see part of the refuge is to follow the Columbia Plateau Trail south from Cheney.

76. Mount Spokane Road

RATING	✹✹✹✹
DISTANCE	22.5 miles
ROAD SURFACE	Paved
ROAD CONDITION	Good
ROAD GRADE	Steep
PUCKER FACTOR	Sightseeing OK
ACCESSIBLE	Summer, fall
LAND MANAGER/CONTACT	Mount Spokane State Park, (509) 238-4258, www.parks.wa.gov
TRAILHEADS	Lower Loop, Upper Loop
CAMPGROUNDS	Bald Knob
NOTES	Discover Pass ($10 daily, $30–$35 annually) required

The Drive

The road to the top of mile-high Mount Spokane leads to a viewpoint where you can look across three states and into Canada.

Getting There

From I-90 in Spokane, take the Division Street exit 281 and drive north on Division to the Y intersection of Highways 2 and 395, bearing right onto Highway 2. Follow Highway 2 for 4.4 miles to Highway 206, the Mount Spokane Road, and turn right. GPS location: N47°47.225'; W117°21.162'

The Road

The road to Mount Spokane has been a favorite of townsfolk ever since Frances Cook built a toll road that reached to within 3.0 miles of the summit, more than 100 years ago. The summit road was completed in the early 1930s and the Civilian Conservation Corps built the beautiful Vista House from native rock on the 5,883-foot peak in 1934. The mountain is the site of the first double chairlift in the world, put into operation in 1947.

Plan this drive on a clear day, which really isn't too hard to do, since summer weather in Eastern Washington means blue sky and sunshine more often than not. Once on the summit, you can see mountain peaks in Idaho, Montana, and British Columbia, and at least six gleaming lakes surrounding the base of the mountain.

Begin by following the Mount Spokane Road east from Highway 2, passing Mount Spokane High School and navigating a totally lame roundabout,

The Vista House atop Mount Spokane was built with native rock by the Civilian Conservation Corps in the 1930s.

following the signs to Mount Spokane State Park. The road crosses Peone Prairie, where farms spread out to the foothills around the mountain. You'll turn north and enter a forested canyon carved by Deadman Creek. The road climbs alongside the creek for several miles.

At **15.0** miles, the road passes by the park entrance, where you can purchase a Discover Pass if you intend to stop anywhere in the park. The road gets a bit steeper, but is well maintained throughout the year. You'll round two switchbacks and climb out of the evergreen forest for views down the mountain to the north and west. At **18.5** miles, arrive at the summit of Linder Ridge and a junction with roads leading to Selkirk Lodge and the Mount Spokane Ski and Snowboard Park. The road to the summit turns left and climbs around Bald Knob Campground at **19.6** miles, where you'll find a picnic area with a shelter and restrooms.

Beyond, the road continues to climb and at **20.3** miles, switches back at a gated road that leads to 5,100-foot Beauty Mountain. You'll head east and

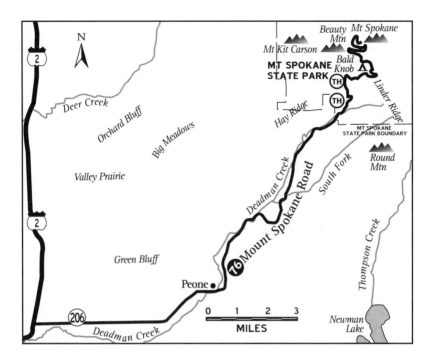

climb along increasingly open slopes to another switchback at the edge of the ski area, switchback again, and finally round the mountain to climb to the summit. There's a wide parking area just below the Vista House, on a short paved trail to the north. Follow the road south from the parking area to a loop around the bald summit, where you'll find sighting tubes pointing to the lakes around the mountain.

77. Mystic Lake

RATING	✪✪✪
DISTANCE	24.6 miles
ROAD SURFACE	Paved/Graded gravel
ROAD CONDITION	Good
ROAD GRADE	Moderate
PUCKER FACTOR	Sightseeing OK
ACCESSIBLE	Summer, fall
TRAILHEADS	Bead Lake
CAMPGROUNDS	Bead Lake, Mystic Lake, Cook's Lake
LAND MANAGER/CONTACT	Colville National Forest, (509) 684-7000, www.fs.fed.us/r6/colville
NOTES	Northwest Forest Pass ($5 daily, $30 annually) required

The Drive
The road past Bead Lake traverses tamarack-filled forests near several small lakes and "diverse" campsites under usually sunny blue skies.

Getting There
From Highway 2 in Newport, cross the Pend Oreille River and turn left on the Le Clerc Road South. Follow it for 2.9 miles to the Bead Lake Road and turn right. GPS location: N48°13.084'; W117°03.462'

The Road
Located near the boundary of the Colville National Forest, Bead Lake is a combination of private homes along one shore and wild forest along the opposite shore, with hiking trails and forest roads stretching to one end of the Y-shaped lake. It's a popular spot for anglers after freshwater lingcod, but those seeking more quiet and solitude can continue farther along a forest road to find both.

Begin by following the paved Bead Lake Road as it transitions from a 50-mile-per-hour speed limit to 35 mph in about 1.0 mile, keeping left at a junction with Bench Road. At **2.3** miles, you'll arrive at a junction with the Marshall Lake Road, and stay left again. The Indian Creek Road leads left to the Geophysical Sno-Park at **3.3** miles, and you'll keep right on the pavement. Next, you'll pass a junction with the Lucky Joe Road at **3.8** miles. Stay left.

At **6.0** miles, you'll enter the Colville National Forest and find a junction with the Bead Lake Ridge Road, Forest Road 3215000. This road climbs to

Lonely Mystic Lake makes a pleasant autumn getaway.

the right and in 0.5 mile, arrives at the lower Bead Lake trailhead. The road continues another 6.0 miles to the upper trailhead, and the trail itself follows the lakeshore and crosses a peninsula for 3.2 miles.

Stay left at the Bead Lake Ridge Road and just beyond, you'll arrive at a junction with a road leading to the Bead Lake Boat Launch on the right. This road leads to the only public access on this end of Bead Lake, a steep, winding road to a launch and parking area above the lake.

Keeping left on the main road, you'll pass the Bead Lake Drive at **7.1** miles and the Crystal Shores Drive at **7.3** miles. Stay left here, passing an unnamed campground on the right and little No Name Lake at **7.9** miles, lost in a forest basin to the right of the road.

Beyond, you'll climb to a big rock quarry on private land, where signs will caution you about blasting in the area. Drive through this work area that borders both sides of the road, which is rocky and bumpy for about 0.25 mile. At **8.2** miles, you'll reenter the forest and keep left at a gated road leading steeply uphill to a mine.

The road now continues through a nice forest of fir and tamarack before passing a recently logged hillside on the left. At **9.4** miles, pass a three-way junction and keep to the middle fork, continuing another 0.5 mile to a private road leading to the left. Stay right and cross back into the Colville National Forest at **11.0** miles.

You'll find the Mystic Lake Road leading to the right at **11.1** miles. This small lake is nestled between forested mountains, 0.6 mile from the junction, and offers several campsites and a restroom above the lake. The lakeshore is pleasant, but can be reached only by a short, very steep, and indistinct trail.

Back at the junction, you'll turn left on Forest Road 5015, the Cook's Lake Road, and at **12.7** miles, pass the Cook's Lake Campground on the left. Cook's Lake is a long, narrow, algae-filled lake with a nice meadow by the campground, which also has a restroom and might make the best picnic spot.

Beyond, FR 5015 joins the Best Chance Road at **15.3** miles, where you'll stay left and leave the forest at **16.3** miles, driving past several private homes and farms. At **21.6** miles, Best Chance Road ends at a junction with the Kings Lake Road. Turn left here and drive 3.0 miles to the community of Usk, crossing the Pend Oreille River and joining Highway 20. You can follow Highway 20 to the south, back to Newport. To bypass Newport, follow Highway 211 just south of Usk and rejoin Highway 2 west of Diamond Lake.

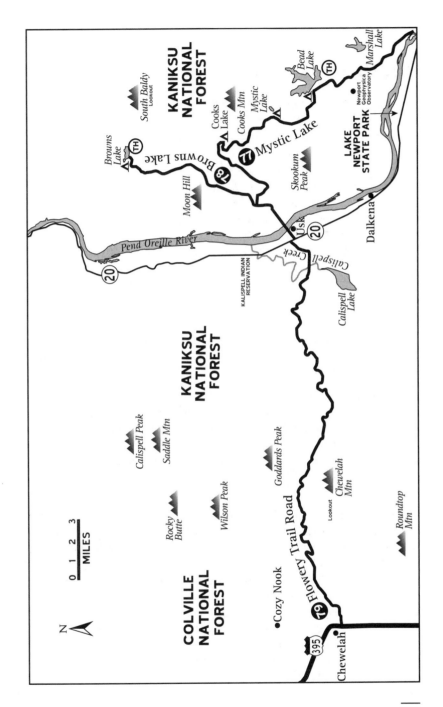

78. Browns Lake

RATING	❀❀❀❀
DISTANCE	11.7 miles
ROAD SURFACE	Paved/Graded gravel
ROAD CONDITION	Good
ROAD GRADE	Moderate
PUCKER FACTOR	Flatlanders welcome
ACCESSIBLE	Summer, fall
TRAILHEADS	Browns Lake Trail
CAMPGROUNDS	Browns Lake
LAND MANAGER/CONTACT	Colville National Forest, (509) 684-7000, www.fs.fed.us/r6/colville
NOTES	Northwest Forest Pass ($5 daily, $30 annually) required

The Drive

The road to Browns Lake rolls through farmland and forest, passing a quiet lake to the site of an old Civilian Conservation Corps camp at a lake that serves up great fly-fishing.

Getting There

From Newport, follow Highway 20 to Usk and turn right on the Kings Lake Road. If you're following Highway 2 from Spokane and wish to bypass Newport, turn left on Highway 211, which rejoins Highway 20 just south of Usk, and turn right on the Kings Lake Road. (See map on page 241.) GPS location: N48°18.599'; W117°17.260'

The Road

The best time to visit Browns Lake is in the fall, after the bugs that feed the big trout in the lake have subsided. Anglers long ago convinced the Forest Service to leave the Browns Lake Campground open later in the fall so they could take advantage of a fishing season that lasts a month beyond the usual Labor Day closing of most National Forest campgrounds in Washington. The lake is open to fly-fishing only.

The drive begins on a paved road that crosses the Pend Oreille River and climbs out of the river valley past ranches and farms for 7.4 miles to the Colville National Forest boundary. In another 0.1 mile, you'll arrive at a junction with the Half Moon Lake Road, Forest Road 5030. Turn left here and continue on the gravel road.

Browns Lake is popular with fly anglers, but offers solitude in the fall.

The route continues to climb in a forest of fir and tamarack, and at **9.4** miles, passes Half Moon Lake on the left. Perhaps you have guessed that this long, narrow lake is shaped like a half moon, though on a map it looks more like a quarter moon. A wide pullout at the north end of the lake makes a good spot to park and walk down to the lakeshore across the byway.

Back on the road, you'll keep right at an unsigned road junction, **11.0** miles from Usk, and right again at a junction with Forest Road 5080. At **11.7** miles, keep left to the Browns Lake Campground. The Civilian Conservation Corps built the cabin at the first campsite in the 1930s. You can park closer to the lake and walk down a fishing boat access road for a lakeshore picnic.

For a long, bumpy, and rocky return on a lesser-used road recommended for vehicles with high ground clearance, you can turn right as you leave the campground on Forest Road 5080, which climbs around the north side of Browns Lake before turning south under 5,988-foot South Baldy Mountain, then descends steeply past North and South Skookum lakes to the junction with the Kings Lake Road, 7.5 miles east of Usk.

79. Flowery Trail Road

RATING	✪✪✪
DISTANCE	27.4 miles
ROAD SURFACE	Paved
ROAD CONDITION	Excellent
ROAD GRADE	Steep
PUCKER FACTOR	Flatlanders welcome
ACCESSIBLE	Year-round
LAND MANAGER/CONTACT	Colville National Forest, (509) 684-7000, www.fs.fed.us/r6/colville
NOTES	Excellent road trip from Spokane for autumn color

The Drive

The Flowery Trail Road climbs over a 4,000-foot mountain pass to one of Eastern Washington's great little ski areas, 49 Degrees North.

Getting There

From Newport, follow Highway 20 north along the scenic Pend Oreille River to the community of Usk and turn left on McKenzie Road. If you're driving from Spokane and wish to bypass Newport, you can follow Highway 2 north to Highway 211 and turn left. Highway 211 joins Highway 20 just south of Usk. Turn left on Highway 20 and left again on McKenzie Road. (See map on page 241.) GPS location: N48°18.599'; W117°17.260'

The Road

It wasn't too long ago that the Flowery Trail Road was closed during the winter just below 4,046-foot-high Flowery Trail Pass at the 49 Degrees North wintersports area. It may not surprise you to know that this great wintersports area is located at N49°. But today, the road is paved and makes a great drive any time of year—and an excellent drive in the fall, when the lowland birch turn sunshine yellow and the tamaracks and aspen glow golden in the high country. Tamaracks, or western larch, drop their soft needles in late fall.

McKenzie Road crosses the flatlands of the Calispell Creek valley before climbing past the West Side Calispell Road, **3.9** miles from Usk. Stay right and continue climbing to the Colville National Forest boundary and the Winchester Road, **7.3** miles from Usk. Continue on the paved Flowery Trail Road to a junction with Forest Road 4347, at **13.7** miles, where the road dips and begins to climb in earnest toward Flowery Trail Pass. At **16.6** miles, pass

Tamarack trees turn golden in the autumn along the Flowery Trail Road.

the entrance to the 49 Degrees North wintersports area on the left and continue another 1.0 mile to the summit of the pass.

You'll pass the entrance to the Chewelah Peak Learning Center on the right at the summit. This Association of Washington School Principals facility hosts as many as 400 students year-round in environmental and outdoor education programs. The summit of Flowery Trail Pass yields a great view to the west of the Colville Valley, more than 2,000 feet below. Tamaracks dominate the forest here and the valley shines like a golden coin in the autumn.

The road now drops in wide switchbacks down into the valley and crosses the forest boundary at **21.6** miles, passing farms and homes before entering the community of Chewelah. Here the Flowery Trail Road joins Highway 395, **27.4** miles from Usk. You can return the way you came or, if you're headed to Spokane, turn left and follow Highway 395 to the south.

80. Salmo Mountain Lookout

RATING	✸✸✸✸✸
DISTANCE	20.9 miles
ROAD SURFACE	Graded gravel
ROAD CONDITION	Good
ROAD GRADE	Steep
PUCKER FACTOR	White knuckles
ACCESSIBLE	Summer, fall
LAND MANAGER/CONTACT	Colville National Forest, Sullivan Lake Ranger District, (509) 446-7500, www.fs.fed.us/r6/colville
TRAILHEADS	Shedroof Divide, Sullivan Lake
CAMPGROUNDS	West Sullivan
NOTES	Rocky, steep drive in final mile

The Drive

This climb to a fire lookout provides views into Idaho and Canada from a beargrass-covered mountaintop.

Getting There

Follow Highway 31 north from Metaline Falls to the Sullivan Lake Road, 2.1 miles, and turn right. Drive 4.5 miles to the Sullivan Creek Road and turn left. GPS location: N48°50.660'; W117°17.228'

The Road

This drive takes you to the very edge of the Salmo-Priest Wilderness, a splendid and lonely forestland on the borders between Washington, Idaho, and British Columbia. It's the home of grizzly bears, moose, elk, and other critters you're not as likely to see in other parts of the state.

Salmo Peak is one of the highest mountains in this neck of the woods, just a few miles from the highest mountain in Eastern Washington—7,309-foot Gypsy Peak to the southwest. The final road to the summit, Forest Road 270, is steep and rough, but can be navigated with care by most any vehicle.

I first visited Salmo Peak to cool off from the hot weather at Sullivan Lake and to find a quieter camp spot. So I drove my truck camper to the flat summit next to the fire lookout, watched an incredible sunset, and wondered if the storm clouds gathering to the northwest might mean lightning and thunder. They did.

Sullivan Creek rages past a diverse campsite along the road to Salmo Lookout.

In a matter of minutes, lightning flashed all around, and I decided the top of a mountain wasn't the safest place to be. I drove to a wide parking area just below the summit and shortly thereafter, a lightning bolt looked as if it hit the lookout tower and thunder shook the truck and camper. It was a great, though frightening adventure.

The paved Sullivan Creek Road, Forest Road 22, turns to gravel just beyond the entrance to the West Sullivan Campground, **0.4** mile from the Sullivan Lake Road. You'll cross Sullivan Creek and turn upstream, passing a number of excellent "diverse" campsites by the creek. At **5.9** miles, arrive at a

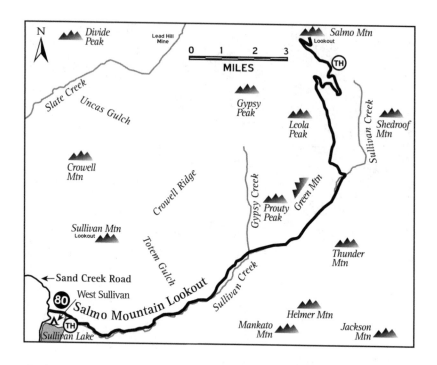

three-way junction and bear left on Forest Road 2220. Follow FR 2220 past a junction at **7.5** miles, staying right.

You've been traveling above the creek, mostly in forest. But at about **12.0** miles, the views begin to open up and you'll turn past Gypsy Meadows and begin climbing more steeply toward Salmo Pass. Stay left at junctions with Forest Roads 280 and 300, **12.6** miles.

After negotiating two switchbacks, at **16.0** and **17.0** miles, you'll arrive at Salmo Pass, **18.7** miles from the Sullivan Lake Road. Turn left, here, and drive 2.2 miles to the lookout. The final 1.0 mile switches back on steep, open slopes with excellent views of the Shedroof Divide to the southwest. Drivers not wishing to make the final, rocky hill to the lookout are welcome to park at the wide area just below, where, I can promise, it's much nicer should a lightning storm brew.

INDEX

More Nature Guides by
SEABURY BLAIR JR.

FOR HIKERS WHO WANT TO TAKE IT EASY

Creaky Knees Guides
Explore the kinder, gentler side of hiking

Features include:
- Trail ratings and information
- Difficulty levels, from a Stroll in the Park to Knee-Punishing
- Driving directions
- Easy-to-read USGS topographical maps

DAY HIKE! THE NORTHWEST'S FAVORITE DAY-HIKING SERIES

Features include:
- Trail ratings
- Difficulty levels, from easy to extreme
- Driving directions
- Easy-to-read USGS topographical maps

Available wherever books are sold

SASQUATCH BOOKS
www.sasquatchbooks.com